BANG YOUR HEAD!

The Real Story of The Missing Link

Dewey "The Missing Link" Robertson
and Meredith Renwick

ECW Press

Published by ECW PRESS
2120 Queen Street East, Suite 200, Toronto, Ontario, Canada M4E 1E2

LIBRARY AND ARCHIVES CANADA CATALOGUING IN PUBLICATION

Robertson, Dewey
Bang your head : the real story of the Missing Link / Dewey Robertson and Meredith Renwick.

ISBN 1-55022-727-0

1. Robertson, Dewey. 2. Wrestlers — Canada — Biography. 3. Wrestlers — Substance use. I. Renwick, Meredith II. Title.

GV1196.R63A3 2006 796.812′092 C2006-900491-9

Editor: Michael Holmes
Cover and Text Design: Tania Craan
Production: Mary Bowness
Printing: Transcontinental

This book is set in Plantin and Aachen

The publication of *Bang Your Head* has been generously supported by the Canada Council, the Ontario Arts Council, and the Government of Canada through the Book Publishing Industry Development Program.

Canadä Canada Council for the Arts Conseil des Arts du Canada

DISTRIBUTION
CANADA: Jaguar Book Group, 100 Armstrong Ave., Georgetown, ON L7G 5S4
UNITED STATES: Independent Publishers Group, 814 North Franklin Street, Chicago, IL 60610

PRINTED AND BOUND IN CANADA

ECW PRESS
ecwpress.com

Contents

FOREWORD

I remember January 16, 1985 vividly. It was my first day working with *Championship Wrestling From Florida*, and my first encounter with Dewey Robertson, "The Missing Link." To say that Dewey is one of the most unique individuals that I have experienced in my 30-plus years in sports entertainment is definitely an understatement. The lessons I learned as his manager while traveling countless miles around the country in one of his old classic green Cadillacs will never be forgotten.

I was honored when Dewey asked me to write the foreword to his autobiography. He sent me an advance manuscript to read, and asked for my suggestions. I made several notes as I read, and realized that it wasn't my place to make any changes to my friend's life story. This is a Byron Robertson chronicle. I tossed my notes into the trash, and returned the book exactly as it was sent to me. However, I must say that I secretly kept something from the package that I addressed to Hamilton, Ontario. I retained a renewed respect for the man known as The Missing Link.

Bang Your Head is as unique as Dewey himself. These chapters document his battles in and out of the professional wrestling ring, and the defeat of the many demons he befriended along the way. His determination and persistence to keep moving forward exemplifies his heart and soul.

Faith, family, and friends are what this personal story is all about. I am so proud to have crossed life's pathways with the author. I am no doubt a better man, and I believe you will walk away from this reading with the exact same sentiments.

Now . . . turn the page and experience Dewey — The Missing Link.

— Percy Pringle III (WWE Legend Paul Bearer)

ACKNOWLEDGMENTS

A lot of people think writing a book is a solitary pursuit. I thought so myself, until Dewey Robertson asked me to help with a project very dear to him, the writing of his autobiography. I knew very little about professional wrestling or the career of Dewey Robertson, but something about his story grabbed my interest when I heard it for the first time, and I thought it would be compelling to a lot of people, wrestling fans or not.

As it is with so many of life's major undertakings, I had no idea what I was getting myself into when I agreed to take on the project. Let's just say it was an adventure, a journey into previously uncharted territory for both myself and Dewey. I learned a lot, and I discovered it takes many people to weave the fabric of a person's life into a coherent pattern. They are part of the story of Dewey's book too, and I'd like to take a moment to acknowledge their contributions.

I was helped immensely by talking to the following people about Dewey's early life, the rise and fall of his career, and his years out of the spotlight following his return to Canada: Killer Tim Brooks, Ragan Davis, Rusty Davis, Harry Demerjian (Ref Harry D — who also provided the funniest account of a Missing Link match I heard from anyone), John Evans (Reginald Love), Jimmy Garvin, Gary Hart, Jimmy Hart, Kevin Hobbs, Ricky Johnson, Gene Lewis, John Mantell, Terry Morgan, Buddy Roberts, Ethel Robertson, Jason Robertson, and Dean Walker.

I also owe a great debt to the fans and historians who've kept the records and the stories of professional wrestling alive — special thanks to Terry Dart and Andrew Calvert for their contributions. A huge thanks also to all the contributors at Kayfabe Memories for providing an invaluable resource when I was trying to piece together where Dewey had been and when.

Other people I owe thanks to are:

Jim Freedman, author of the superb *Drawing Heat* (it's hard to find, but well worth the effort) for his insights into the nature of Dewey's appeal to wrestling fans past and present.

Britt Britton, promoter of Wrestlecon, for putting The Link back in the public eye and giving me a chance to meet some of the other wrestlers of World Class Championship Wrestling.

Bill Hanna and Matie Molinaro, for their guidance and advice on writing books and navigating the publishing industry.

And finally, a heartfelt thanks to my husband, Greg Oliver, for his patience, love and support, for his role in raising the standards for writing about professional wrestling, and most of all for encouraging me when I was ready to hand the whole project over to someone else. As always, you were right.

— Meredith Renwick

DEDICATION

To my family, who should have come first — for so many reasons. I hope you'll understand a little better when you're done reading this.

To Dean Walker, a man who never quits, and who heard me tell my story at a school and first encouraged me to write it down.

To Paul Pendakis, Angelo DiAnia, and the many 12-step groups who invited me to share my story in many venues — public schools, high schools, service clubs, jails — so I could help others from starting down the wrong path.

To Susan Brower, widow of Dick "The Bulldog" Brower, who was instrumental in getting me started and directing me to the extraordinary Matie Molinaro, who listened to and advised me for ten years.

To Wayne Harrison, fan, friend and the person who for ten years made me believe this project was worthwhile.

To Kevin Hobbs, friend, writer, fan and wrestler.

To Bill Puskas, lifetime friend and training partner.

To Keith Adams, fan and friend.

To Gene "Cousin Luke" Lewis, who was always ready to share his optimism.

To all the employers, promoters and bookers who kept me working for 44 years and always gave me a break.

To all the other 12-steppers, doctors, fans, mentors and friends who listened, gave advice, and helped me get back on the road to recovery when I strayed. You know who you are.

To the memory of all the wrestlers whose lives have been tragically cut short by the abuses that nearly took me down. They are sadly missed by their peers, fans and families, but will never be forgotten.

Prologue

FOR THE LINK

Where does he come from?
Nobody knows.
Where is he going?
To parts unknown.
Can Sheena control him?
He pulls at his hair,
He does not speak
The General is there.
What does he feel as he bangs his head?
His opponents shiver, and wish they were dead.

Does he come from a jungle,
Where they walk on all fours?
Or a far-off planet,
In between all the stars?
He's fierce and ferocious,
So better beware.
Stay out of the ring
If The Missing Link is there.

Diane, June, 1984

The two photographers were in the empty dressing room backstage at the University of Tampa Spartan Sports Center. They were waiting for a professional wrestler called The Missing Link, to see if they could take his picture for an upcoming issue of *Sports Illustrated.* Long regarded as a cartoonish pseudo-sport ranked a notch or two above a carnival freak show, in the spring of 1985 professional wrestling had suddenly become trendy. A promoter based in New York City named Vince McMahon Jr. had just put on a huge, star-studded extravaganza called *WrestleMania* at Madison Square Garden that made a lot of money and was seen by over a million people via closed-circuit television, the largest audience ever for a single wrestling show. McMahon's World Wrestling Federation, as he called it, had also created the celebrity athlete of the moment, a blond-mustached, yellow-spandex-clad giant named Hulk Hogan who was getting the full star treatment from the mainstream media. *Sports Illustrated* had decided that despite its dodgy claim to being a sport, professional wrestling was now worthy of a cover story. The photographers had gone to Georgia first, where there was another longstanding, very successful wrestling promotion but got an extremely hostile reception from the management there, so they came further south to Florida.

The dressing room had been full of people when they arrived, mostly hard-core fans and other wrestlers, who were brusquely hustled away by security and The Missing Link's bodyguards before they entered. "What are you doing? Get your hands off me," shouted one female fan as she was escorted out. "What's the problem? We're supposed to be here," insisted another. "Not tonight, you're not," replied the bodyguard. "Now get out."

The photographers had no idea what to expect when The Missing Link arrived in the dressing room. The Link was a strange character even in the out-there world of professional wrestling. He had a honed, 260-pound bodybuilder's physique, but that was combined with a blue-and-green painted face, a bizarre tufted hairdo and a beard like a malevolent circus clown. His hair was black; he wore black trunks and furry black boots with matching knee and elbow pads. And if The Link's appearance was weird, his behavior was downright scary. He was like a primitive Neanderthal man come back to life in the 20th century. The Link had never spoken a word to anyone in the ring or out of it, and often appeared not to know where he was or what he was doing there. During matches he would wander aimlessly around staring at the ring floor, growling softly to himself like a jungle cat, occasionally stopping to glance up in a startled way at the crowd, never looking his opponents in the eye. Just when they thought he'd forgotten they were there, without warning The Link would rear up, grab the tuft of hair on the back of his head, let out a terrifying roar, charge headfirst at his opponent's chest and the match would be on.

That particular night The Missing Link climbed out of the ring when his match was over, trudging down the narrow aisle, his eyes cast down on the ground. He occasionally stopped and jerked his head upward to glance at the fans, many of whom had blue-and-green painted faces identical to his. Suddenly a fan jumped out in front of him and handed him a metal folding chair. The Link knew instinctively what the fans wanted to see. He grabbed the chair in both hands, raised it up in the air and pounded the chair against his skull again and again, so hard it dented the chair seat, while the cheers got louder with each blow. The Link's hard head was his most fearsome weapon in the ring. Besides using it to knock down other wrestlers, he would slam it into chairs, tables, turnbuckles, even ring stairs (sometimes until his forehead was bloody) without ever showing any sign that it hurt him.

Backstage, the dressing room door opened and in came a slim, attractive dark-haired woman dressed all in black — leather chauffeur's cap, tight-fitting blouse, spandex pants and high-heeled shoes. This was The Link's driver and handler Sheena, who went everywhere with him. She was the only person The Link would listen to — even his manager, the perpetually furious, spluttering, motor-mouthed Percival Pringle III, could not always make The Link behave. Sheena would guide The Link backstage after the shows, taking him by the arm every time he was distracted by the crowd and moving him towards the dressing room. Now the green-faced behemoth the two photographers had been waiting for stood in the doorway behind Sheena, obviously hesitant to enter his dressing room with strangers in it. Sheena looked at the two men and asked "Who are you?"

"We're from *Sports Illustrated.* We're here to take The Link's picture," said one of the men. "Great!" Sheena replied. "We'd love to have you take his picture." She drew The Link into the room and the photographers looked at him. Any expectations that he might drop out of the character and turn back into a normal person evaporated as they watched him. The Link stood mutely with his shoulders hunched forward, muscular arms slightly extended as though he was looking for a club or a large animal bone to grab, eyes trained on the ground. They had taken pictures of many athletes and entertainers but never anyone this intimidating. If it was an act, it was an extremely effective one. "Could you get him to do one of his wild poses for us?" one man finally asked Sheena.

"I don't know, that might be difficult," she mused. "He doesn't like to be given orders on how to behave. In fact, he doesn't even like having his picture taken." She thought a bit longer. "I know!" she said. "I'll whisper something to him, and when he gets upset you be ready to take a picture, quick." They focused their cameras as she leaned over and spoke into The Link's ear, something only he could hear. He came to life immediately. His head snapped up, his hand went to the back of his head, he leaned back and opened his eyes and mouth wide and let out the roar that other wrestlers had learned to fear. The photographers had their picture.

The "Mat Mania!" issue of *Sports Illustrated* hit the newsstands on April 29, 1985. Hulk Hogan was on the cover, but The Missing Link's picture was the centerfold. A couple of weeks later, The Link was on his way to New York and the World Wrestling Federation.

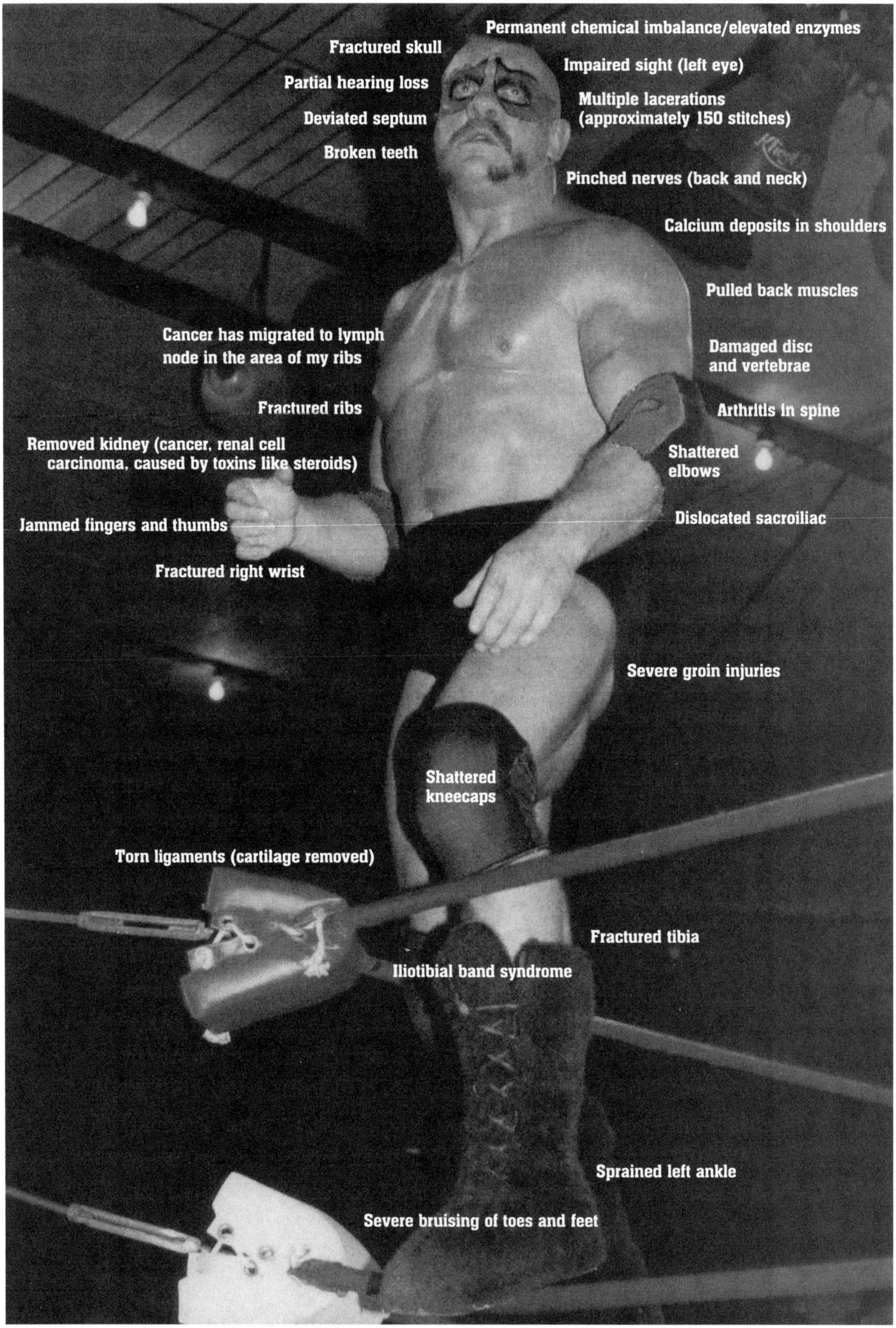
Permanent chemical imbalance/elevated enzymes
Fractured skull
Impaired sight (left eye)
Partial hearing loss
Multiple lacerations (approximately 150 stitches)
Deviated septum
Broken teeth
Pinched nerves (back and neck)
Calcium deposits in shoulders
Pulled back muscles
Cancer has migrated to lymph node in the area of my ribs
Damaged disc and vertebrae
Fractured ribs
Arthritis in spine
Removed kidney (cancer, renal cell carcinoma, caused by toxins like steroids)
Shattered elbows
Jammed fingers and thumbs
Dislocated sacroiliac
Fractured right wrist
Severe groin injuries
Shattered kneecaps
Torn ligaments (cartilage removed)
Fractured tibia
Iliotibial band syndrome
Sprained left ankle
Severe bruising of toes and feet

CHAPTER ONE

The Man Behind the Blue-and-Green Mask

Hi. My name is Dewey Robertson, and I used to be The Missing Link.

This book is the story of my life, my career in wrestling and my struggle with addiction to steroids, alcohol and drugs — the good, the bad and the ugly. Recovery from addiction is without question the toughest match I've ever fought. I am not writing this book to tell you what to do. I am just going to tell you what happened to me, and hope that people learn from it.

For nearly 15 years I was the "All-Canadian Boy" of professional wrestling. I was one of the most versatile faces in the business; my good friend, the late Bullwhip Danny Johnson called me "The Man of a Thousand Moves." As a dedicated bodybuilder since the age of 19 and someone who was always extremely conscientious about what I put into my body, I never thought I would become a substance abuser of any kind. Even now my mother says to me, "Byron" (that's my real name), "I don't ever remember you drinking a lot. You were always so interested in your health." That's true. If I drank at all, it was in moderation — two or three beers to loosen up at a party, never any more. I weight-trained and wrestled without using any steroids or illicit drugs for many years. That all changed when I moved to Charlotte, North Carolina, in the late 1970s. While going to Charlotte gave a huge boost to my wrestling career, I was also introduced to steroids and my drug of choice, marijuana. Once I left Canada, it only took 13 years of steroids, alcohol and drugs to take me to the bottom — and I mean the bottom.

When times were good it seemed harmless, but after a few years I came to a point when my career had stalled and I had to take drastic action. I went to Texas, shaved my head, painted my face and changed my name to The Missing Link. The Link was an immediate sensation, drawing so much heat that riots sometimes broke out during shows. But nobody knew that the outrageous antics everyone loved so much — the roaring, the hair-grabbing, the headbutts and chair-smashing — were fueled by my growing addiction to steroids, alcohol and drugs. The Link saved my wrestling career, but he nearly killed Dewey Robertson in the process. I literally "went missing" as The Link took over my personality. I lived the gimmick 24 hours a day. I didn't speak to anyone for nearly eight years and sank into a fog of addiction.

As my mind and body went downhill, so did my career. When the last promotion I worked for went out of business in the late 1980s, reality hit me with devastating force. I was approaching my 50th birthday with no money, no career and nothing but my customized Linkmobile truck to my name. I had nothing to fall back on, because I hadn't saved a cent. All of my money had been spent on living the high life.

After a long, humbling struggle with poverty, illness and homelessness, my family and I finally made our way back to Canada and began to rebuild our lives from the bottom up. I had to go into rehab, and then recovery, which has been my primary occupation for the last 16 years or so. I've stayed sober, but not always clean, and it's a constant battle to stay on track. My biggest challenge came when my wife left me after 32 years of marriage and I wasted a lot of time afterwards thinking she would come back to me — time that should have been spent getting on with the rest of my life. She never came back, and why should she? I blamed her for every mistake I made. It's a credit to her that she hung in as long as she did. I hope one day she'll be able to forgive me for all the terrible things I did while we were married.

As for me, I'm still wrestling occasionally, trying to achieve a measure of serenity and repair the damage that years of drinking and drug use did to my family life. I do a lot of public speaking about my experiences with addiction and recovery. Most importantly, I am finally starting to learn the lesson that in order to move on, I have to accept the past and then let go of it. And that's what I hope to do by writing this book. There may be mistakes in here — my memory isn't what it used to be — but this is the story the way I remember it.

* * *

I have an album of childhood photographs my mother gave to me as a Christmas present in the early 1970s that I enjoy looking through when I'm feeling down. There's photos of my grandfather, my mother and pretty well everybody else in the family holding me as a baby; my father holding me on a pony, standing on the running board of his old Ford, wearing his army uniform, with his army platoon. Some of the photos were taken at my house and some taken four doors up the street where my grandmother lived. I can see the years going by and me growing older: sitting on Santa Claus's knee, class photos with three rows of kids in front of the school, pictures taken on holidays, as a teenager, and at friends' wedding ceremonies.

The pictures tell me a story: that both my parents and my grandparents loved me very much, that I had a lot of friends, and how important it is to have something that reminds you of the good times, because life goes on very rapidly sometimes and changes happen that we don't expect. That album tells me these were moments in my life I enjoyed very much, and I shouldn't forget them when I think about all the bad things I've been through. A lot of people who are in recovery don't grow up the way I did. Usually they come from abusive homes — they find the glass on the table when they're 11 or 12 years old, take a drink of what's in it and it makes the pain go away for a while. That's not how it happened for me.

I was born Byron James John Robertson on February 28, 1939 to Ethel and Ken Robertson, of West Hamilton, Ontario, Canada. At that time, West Hamilton was a little village of its own, separate from the city of Hamilton. It was tucked under the mountain, across from where McMaster University Hospital is now. My brother Ken was born four years after me. I'm sorry to say I can't tell you much about him. When things started to go bad between my parents, I began spending most of my time out of the house and never got to know my brother very well. This is only one of many regrets I have now about the direction my life eventually took.

I wouldn't say we were poor but like everybody else back then, we made do with much less than people today would consider necessary for a good life. It was a simpler time. Parents, peers and neighborhood friendships helped form a stable community for everyone. The kinds of activities kids have today weren't available, but we valued what we did have. The Saturday movie matinee with its continuing serial was very important, along with TV, and family-oriented activities like picnics, which usually included immediate family, relatives and friends. I think a lot of people have lost this sense of community today, and maybe we should be thinking about ways to try and bring it back, because it's so important for developing character and responsibility.

I got the nickname "Dewey" when I was about nine years old. A friend of mine, a boy named Howard from a block away who I went to school with, just started calling me Dewey one day. I have no idea where he got it from. I would go home and tell my dad "They keep calling me Dewey" and my dad would say "Don't answer them," but I never did get rid of the name. The funny thing is, when I got into wrestling, most wrestlers change their real names but I just used the name Dewey and ended up keeping it, and I've been very happy with it all my life. My mother and the odd person I've known since childhood call me Byron, but not too many people know me as Byron anymore.

When I look back at my childhood, thoughts about my father are the heaviest in my heart. He was divorced by my mother when I was 14 years old, and died in 1972. To this day, I think of how much I loved him but never had a chance to tell him. He worked for the Hamilton Street Railway as a bus driver. I remember him as a quiet, very kind man, who was never loud and was liked by everybody. I must have respected him myself, because to this day I don't ever remember getting spanked, just maybe a boot in the behind, with little contact, on the way to my bedroom and being told to stay there.

The few things that I did with my dad are still with me today. He would dig a few holes in the backyard and practice chipping golf balls with me. Golf is probably the first sport I played, and it is now back in my life again. He would wrestle with me on the floor all the time, and spent many hours teaching me about boxing. I had toy pistols and cap guns like all young children back then, and my father used his army training to teach me how to shoot at a target and from the hip. He taught me to drive his old Ford, always took me with him when he went to visit his mother in Dundas, or my other grandmother who lived four doors from us. They would spend their time talking and enjoying themselves, but always drinking wine. This is important, because as I got older arguments about his drinking became a nightly occurrence between him and my mother, and eventually led to a divorce.

But most of all, my father knew hockey was so important to me that he would drive me and the other guys from the Golden Eagles, a neighborhood club I belonged to, from West Hamilton to the old Barton Street arena at 5:30 in the morning to practice or play. My dream at that time, like most Canadian boys, was to be a hockey player. I wanted to be a pro with the Detroit Red Wings. I remember going to the Royal Connaught Hotel as a teenager during the pre-season NHL hockey and getting autographs from the Red Wing players — Bob Golden, Terry Sawchuk, Red Kelly, Gordie Howe — when they were in town to play the annual game against their farm team, the Hamilton Red Wings.

I started to tell you about my father's drinking. My memories of that begin from when I was about ten years old. My brother and I had to share a single bed, and I would lie there listening to my parents arguing late at night when my father would get home from a night of drinking beer at the local hotel. It was obvious to me even then that my father didn't want to come home to my mother. I don't know why. I remember my mother as a loving woman, but obviously his drinking was upsetting her. I would listen to her nagging and nagging, saying "You got a chip on your shoulder." I didn't know what that meant then, and I still don't. My mother won't talk about it now. Other nights I would have to go out myself around midnight, to the corner which was a couple of lots away from the houses, where someone would let my father off from the hotel. He would either be stumbling along or crawling and I would have to help him get home.

Around this time I began going outside my immediate family for activities and role models that would help me cope with what was happening at home. I spent a lot of time with my maternal grandmother. She had a TV which showed pro wrestling from Chicago weekly, after the 11 o'clock news. The shows were broadcast live from the Chicago Amphitheater. Jack Brickhouse was the announcer, and he also did the interviews with the wrestlers. We would watch with awe as the good and bad guys faced each other in the ring and played with the emotions of the crowd. We felt the intimidation that wrestlers projected during their interviews as they growled, scowled, blamed and threatened their opponents with incredible wit and false accusations. I was told by someone a long time ago that everyone identifies with wrestling because from the time we are born, our bodies never stay still. Learning to crawl, learning to walk, playing with toys, wrestling with brothers and sisters or other children, our arms and legs are always moving from the time we are infants. Then as we get older, we don't get to roughhouse as much with other people, so I think that's one thing that draws people to watch professional wresting. And there was the emotional release that comes from identifying with and cheering on the heel or babyface — whether they were in the arena with the lights down or in their living room, people could feel free to let their inner feelings go with nobody judging them. I also think that for me, wrestling provided an outlet for all the troubled emotions I was having about my parents fighting. But I was not yet imagining that one day I would be one of those guys in the ring. It was strictly a schoolboy fantasy then.

One area of my life that really suffered from all the turmoil at home was school. I could not focus on my work at all, and sometimes I would even fall asleep at my desk. I didn't get much help at home with my studies either, so I never learned to do homework. From kindergarten to grade eight, I failed five times. There wasn't anybody that got the strap more than me, and I can't tell you why. I was not a troublemaker, I was timid, I was an introvert, so why did this happen? My interests went to shop, physical education and participation in all sports. I lived for sports, but academic success eluded me. The only time I was ever happy was when I was out with a hockey stick or baseball or at the park.

I know most of the problem was plain old tiredness from being up late every night, but I also think now that academic subjects always held less interest for me than the people who taught me. I was looking for people to take the place of my parents, who were caught up in their own troubles and not able to give me the guidance I was looking for. I still remember the many peers and adults from that time in my life that I admired and tried to emulate. Learning is a never-ending process, and the influence of good people is equally as important as any other ingredient. I really looked up to any adults who were in high-profile positions — service club members, school principals or anybody who had knowledge that I wanted to listen to — as mentors. And I was easy enough to get along with, so people would really share with me, and I think that's where, if at all, any education that I had came from. Listening to what these mentors said to me created a sense of responsibility in me that led to my successes later on.

I was about 11 years old when I started caddying at the Hamilton Golf & Country Club on weekends. My friend Joe Cheesman and I would stand just in front of McMaster University and hitchhike to the club at 5:30 in the morning. This was to get our names in on the list of caddies in order to get out early and maybe carry a bag on a second round that same afternoon. Also, if we got to the golf course just after sunrise, sometimes we'd be allowed to play on the three-hole practice course. This was very important, because it kept us busy and allowed us to practice all the rules of etiquette that we would learn from the members while caddying during the day. And most importantly, we learned how to mix, play with and get along with other boys that came from other parts of Hamilton and the surrounding areas.

There were grades of caddies: AA, A, B, and C. Joe and I started as C caddies and made 65 cents for 18 holes. HGCC also had a caddy master, whose job it was to keep about 80 young boys quiet at that time of the morning. While the members would tee off on the first hole just in front of the pro shop, we caddies were about 40 yards away around the corner, anxiously waiting to go out.

It was on weekdays, or when things were slow, that the caddy master taught us the most important lessons. That was when he would take us to the three-hole practice course — nowadays they have driving ranges — to teach us how to stake out, stand or hold the pin properly while the member was putting, wash the golf balls and retrieve the balls. We learned to discuss golf, distances, the choice of clubs with a member and, most of all, good manners. All of that came with practice, along with patience and responsibility — members would often ask you to carry their wallets — integrity, proper etiquette and a chance to develop your personality. In the next four years, Joe and I moved up to be AA caddies, earning $4.50 for carrying two bags each for one round (18 holes). On Saturday or Sunday we'd caddy two rounds a day.

Probably the best thing that came out of the experience is that near the end of the season HGCC ran a golf tournament, allowing the younger caddies to play on the club's small course and the older caddies to use the large and very lavish course. This event was the first part of one of the most important things in my life. It was highlighted by the caddy banquet held in their beautiful clubhouse, and on that evening I was presented with a cash prize of $70, just like a real golf tournament. They also had a guest speaker, the actor Gordie Tapp. Even at that young age, I remember how much I admired him because he could get up and speak in front of people, and I always visualized myself as a keynote speaker one day — as good as Gordie Tapp was if not better — someone people would listen to and admire. That was one dream that stayed with me, and I'm still working towards it many years later.

Golf was the first of many sports that was really important to me, and sometimes I wish I'd stayed with it, but once my final season ended, I had to go to work and help my mother support the family. I still have golfing dreams: to play with John Daly, and to be accepted by the HGCC as a speaker. I've gone back to that golf club recently and they haven't accepted me yet, but they will someday.

I mentioned a neighborhood club I belonged to, The Golden Eagles. Started sometime around 1951-52, The Golden Eagles were just a group of neighborhood boys who loved sports, and we kept ourselves very active playing basketball, swimming, and floor and ice hockey. We were encouraged and supported by the West Hamilton Kiwanis International and a man named Keith Smith, the director of the Hamilton downtown YMCA, who was the organizer and our older brother/close friend. He taught us how to run our club by having meetings alternately at our homes, electing officers, collecting dues to buy jackets, sweaters and pay for ice rental. We mostly used the local gym at Princess Elizabeth Public School or the Hamilton Downtown YMCA.

Keith Smith also arranged for me to spend the summer at YMCA Camp Wanakita, ten miles outside of Haliburton, when I was about 13. I went there as a junior camper who couldn't swim and who had never been camping in his life. They kept me dry all summer as staff groundskeeper, which mainly meant keeping the kyboes (outhouses, toilets) in good working order.

I ended up going for three summers. Next season I was made

a junior counselor and lifeguarding was added to my duties. The lifeguards stood on a raft about 40 yards out in the water, and I had to be taken out by the lifeboat because I still couldn't swim. By my third summer at Camp Wanakita I was a senior counselor and not only had I learned to swim, I had five YMCA swim cards, my Royal Lifesaving and a Bronze Medallion Award. I also had a master canoeing certificate and became a Voyager, which entailed going on five- and ten-day canoe trips, including portaging. Not bad for a kid who'd been a non-camper just a few years earlier!

Unfortunately, none of these character-building experiences had any effect on my performance in school. I finally gave up and left after grade nine. By then I was 15, I had been the senior counselor at YMCA camp for the summer and after that got offered a full-time job in the pro shop at the golf course, so I saw no point in continuing with school. This didn't seem like a big deal to me at the time, as I knew I had no aptitude for academic work, but not having a lot of formal education did limit the kind of jobs I was able to get later on. Nowadays kids really do need to stay in school if they want to get anywhere in life.

Even though I wasn't any good at school, I was still able to learn a lot from people I associated with and looked up to as role models. Here's one that I'll never forget: during my teenage years I lived about ten houses down from a boy a few years older than me who was an outstanding athlete as well as an honor student. He excelled at all the sports: basketball, hockey, baseball and football. We spent countless hours throwing baseballs and footballs back and forth, and I would swear to this day on a stack of Bibles that he threw to me more times than to anybody else in his long career. He threw the baseball low, high — sometimes so high it seemed to be a mile in the air or with such speed it was frightening, showing me that it was just the snap of the wrist after the arm was extended that made the difference. He could play any position, and he turned down a number of offers from American pro baseball leagues. With a football he could already throw the low, *flat* pass that made him number one. He'd make me run long and fast, but I could rarely catch up to his throw. I was not yet at my full height and still very skinny.

When he began his incredible pro sports career I followed it closely. In the 12 years he played for the Ottawa Rough Riders he was a multiple award winner, including Grey Cup Champion and Most Outstanding Player. He's a holder of numerous CFL records, a Canadian Football Hall of Famer, Member of the Order of Canada. But what I remember best is the early example he set for me, because I learned from him that there would be a place in professional sports for me one day too. If you haven't guessed it already, his name was Russ Jackson — and I would like to thank you now, Russ, for your time and the inspiration you gave to me.

⋆ ⋆ ⋆

After I had worked all season in the HGCC pro shop, a club member asked me to work for a wholesale hardware store in Hamilton, Wilkinson-Compass. From Wilkinson-Compass, which allowed me to get my driver's license, I started driving a small tractor-trailer for a local haulage company, Cargo Transit, and I was in and out of Stelco, one of Hamilton's major steel manufacturers, quite often. That enticed me to apply for a job there and I worked at Stelco for the next three years.

The day I started working at the age of 15, I made $29 a week and my mother took $15 of that as rent to help our situation. I have to admit I resented her doing that, but it's important that kids today know I had to contribute at home. She remarried after the divorce, but her second husband was a sick man and she had to go out to work as a waitress at the McMaster Teacher's College to support us financially. I suppose her second husband was a good man, but I had very little to do with him. I just wanted my own father back.

I also have to say I was very angry at my mother because of the divorce, and that anger lasted a long time. In fact, I'm still struggling with it today. After she told my father to leave, I started distancing myself from her, didn't confide in her or tell her much about my life outside the home. I paid my rent to her every week, but that was about it. I know she cared for me — she always told me she loved me and taught me to not to lie or steal, to be responsible and polite to people — but I still have a lot of negative thoughts about her and my childhood. I realize now that I was very envious of other people, maybe because I felt they had a lot more to offer me than my own family. I almost didn't want to write that down, but I realize it's a truth I have to face if I ever want to let go of my anger. The point I'm trying to make is when I carried on and made gains in sports and working hard at the jobs I took on, I usually excelled because these were things that I had this powerful drive to succeed at, and it came from being frustrated at our poverty and the loss of control I felt when my father was taken away from me.

As I said earlier, my father died when I was still fairly young. It was in 1972 when I was living down in Shreveport, Louisiana, wrestling for Tri-State. After the divorce he remarried too, and had another child. He was pretty much out of my life and my thoughts until I went into recovery. I did see my father occasionally after the divorce, but my mother's experience made me feel that he was a bad person, so I wasn't very nice to him, and I'm very sorry for that now. As time went on, I'd see him and he wouldn't recognize me because of his drinking. It's not till you get older that you realize the importance of forgiveness, and sometimes that knowledge comes too late. It's a very touchy issue, and I hope it's all cleansed one day.

But at the time, all my energy was going towards work, and

sports. I had a full-time job at Stelco, I continued to play hockey and worked as a lifeguard in the summers. I had a good friend from Camp Wanakita named Rusty Davis — his brother had been the swimming instructor for the whole camp, and thus was responsible for me becoming qualified to lifeguard in the first place. Rusty and I worked weekends together at a small beach at the Brant Inn in Burlington. There was about 50 yards of beachfront, it wasn't very deep, and every Saturday morning we'd rake it and all weekend people would have a nice place to swim and enjoy themselves.

There was a crew of about eight to 12 lifeguards, all big guys, and I was trying to bulk myself up like the rest of them. I was tall — 6'2" — but only weighed about 140 pounds, and all the other guys were probably 200 pounds or more, so I'd always bring a lot of food with me to eat during the day. I remember eating lots of bananas, large lunches and desserts. Rusty says he remembers me eating chocolate cake and drinking chocolate milk at 8 o'clock in the morning and doing my pushups and sit-ups in the sun. I can't say this was an officially sanctioned training diet, I just tried to eat whatever I thought would help me gain weight. I had lots of energy but no physical size, because in our house one steak would feed four people.

I was finding my lack of size extremely frustrating for my budding hockey career too. At that time I was playing hockey for Dundas Grafton's Intermediate A hockey team, with my eye on the Hamilton Red Wings. I was playing a game in Dunnville when a few of us got involved in a skirmish right up against the boards. My back was to the boards, and a fan I never even saw reached over, grabbed the back of my jersey and lifted me right off the ice. I was powerless. I don't believe anybody else saw this incident, but I never forgot it, and I knew I would have to gain some serious weight if I wanted to continue.

When I was about 19 years old, I heard about a bodybuilding

and wrestling gym on King and West Avenue in downtown Hamilton, run by a former British Empire wrestling champion, and decided to check it out. I thought I was just going there to learn how to build my body up. Little did I know I was about to alter the direction of my life forever.

CHAPTER TWO

"It's Up to You"

Al Spittles' Gym

These were my measurements when I started bodybuilding:

Chest: 35"
Bicep: 10-1/2"
Forearm: 11"
Thighs: 20"
Neck: 14-1/2"
Shoulder: 42"
Weight: about 144

Pretty scrawny, huh? But by the time I was 24, I weighed 238 pounds, and I did it the old-fashioned way. I trained hard, ate properly, got lots of sleep, and in the process found the career direction I'd been looking for.

When I arrived at Al Spittles' Gym for the first time, I found an old building on the corner of King and West Avenue, a very busy part of Hamilton, with a second-storey window where Al would sit watching people hurry past. If Al wasn't in the window he was in the far back corner, looking out on an old-style gym with iron weights, dumbbells and barbells, and wooden homemade benches, all circling something that I had no idea would enter my life yet. It was a homemade wrestling ring, a 16-foot squared circle that rose to about four inches above the floor. It used four steel posts that were part of the building's structure — perfect components to put up ropes with lots of spring to them, as adapting to the ropes was very important for many moves, plus timing. The gym always had veterans in both wrestling and bodybuilding around too, so it was a great place to get good advice on training.

I was very impressed with Al, who was a former professional wrestler himself. His real name was Al Spittles, but he had wrestled as Al Hamilton, and held the British Heavyweight Wrestling Title in England under that name — the same title that was later was won by Whipper Billy Watson and brought back to Canada from England, where he retired with it. I guessed Al was probably in his mid-50s then. He was about the same height as I was, 6'1"– 6'2", always held his head up high, and had a very sharp vocabulary. He reminded me of my grade school shop teacher, who was stern, crisp and blunt but always spoke with much wisdom.

The conditions of Al's Gym may sound roughshod, but I think it truly was the type of environment that makes one put forth his best efforts. Between Al's gym, the Jewish Centre and Jack Wentworth's gym, the city of Hamilton became known in the wrestling world as The Factory because so many top-class wrestlers came out of these training facilities. Here's a "short" list of names who got their start in Hamilton: Ivan Koloff; John and Chris Tolos; Steve Bolus; Jerry Aiken; Jack Hill (The Assassin); Ernie Moore; Wes Hutchings and John Evans (The Love Brothers); The Kelly Twins; Billy Red Lyons (my future tag partner, friend and best mentor); Bill Terry (Kurt Von Hess); George and Sandy Scott; Nick DiCarlo; Vic Rossitani; "Mr. Hamilton" Angelo Mosca, plus his son; Hurricane and Cyclone Smith; Terry Yorkston; Bull Johnson; Danny Johnson; Martin Hutzler; Ben and Mike Sharpe (World Tag Champions); Paul DeMarco; John Quinn; Murray Cummings; Benny Lima (also a great trainer); Matt Gilmore (another of my trainers); Ernie Schwab; Bill White; Mike Dockman; Andy Martin; Eric the Red; Danny Little Bear; Terry Morgan; and Johnny Powers. My apologies to those names that are missing, but I could fill up a whole book just with Hamilton wrestlers. Later, when I went on the road myself, every dressing room I entered would have at least one other Hamiltonian in it. Even when I was The Missing Link and Frank Tunney was helping to promote New York, the Hamilton locals still kept coming.

When I started at Al's in 1958, it cost $10 a month to join the gym, and you worked out three days a week. I started the weight training program, and Al showed me the basic exercises I would be doing. I don't even think it was on a card system — he just took you around and showed you what to do. There was a weight-lifting platform at one end of the gym where I learned the three basic lifts: the press, clean and jerk, and the hardest lift of all, the overhead snatch. Al told me this was the best way to learn timing, speed and strength. After he thought you had it down, Al would sit at his desk and watch, or he might come over and stand beside you to encourage you while you were doing your squats. You did them with a bar on your shoulders and he kept pushing you and also supporting you. Or if you were on the bench press, he would come to spot you there. Al's favorite saying was "It's up to you." I can hear him still — "It's up to you, it's up to you" would ring in your ear the whole time and that would keep you going.

It didn't take long to master these exercises, because I did the same ones all the time. Then I started learning new exercises from the guys who had been around the gym for a while. I found myself attending this gym with a flood of other young men in their early 20s, who came from Kitchener, Hamilton, Dundas, Caledonia, Niagara Falls and Welland.

I guess Al liked me because he always kept his eye on me and made lots of comments to help improve my new-found training skills. Maybe it was my keen interest and regular attendance that he liked. Over the years workout equipment has changed and improved but the training methods and concepts are still relevant. The equipment was all free weights back then, no machines. Some of the weights would hook up to pulleys and cables, but it would have free weights on it, not a stack of weights. The exercises we did were all basically the same exercises that people do today. Just the other day I worked out on a new leg machine at my gym and thought *Wow, have these ever come a long way.* But it's still exactly the same exercise I used to do at Al's all those years ago.

When I joined Al's gym I was working in the nails division at Stelco, which was a very noisy and dirty job. Because nails are stamped out with hundreds of machines going at one time, it required wearing protection, and a lot of grease was needed to keep the machines running smoothly. I also had to stack the 106-pound kegs of nails, and stack them quite high, which required a lot of strength.

There were four wrestlers working at Stelco when I was there, and two of them were in the nails division with me, Bill and Jim Rawlings. They had been champions in England and came to Canada to live, and I remember them showing me their wrestling moves. One of them used to just pick me up and press me over his head. I think knowing these wrestlers was probably a factor in my eventual decision to direct myself towards wrestling when

I started training at Al's. I knew I didn't want to work for Stelco the rest of my life.

After three months of regular workouts at Al's, I was starting to notice an improvement in the way I looked and felt. A lot of people get themselves motivated to start training and quit after a few weeks, but if you can get three months in, that's usually enough time for it to get a hold on you. I was busy absorbing the three basic concepts of a healthy body: nutrition, rest and training. Eating right is as important as putting the proper kind of gas in your car. I read bodybuilding magazines for diet tips, as they were the only source of nutritional information available then. Most of my information came from these magazines, which had write-ups on bodybuilders, training programs and diet programs.

After I had been training for a while, I read in one of the magazines about a guy named Bruce Randall, from Columbus, Ohio, who ate more than a dozen eggs, 12 bananas, and drank five quarts of milk a day. I started following the same diet but I could only drink four-and-a-half quarts of milk a day. And I was really motivated to gain weight, so that shows you how hard it is. Sometimes I would be lying in bed at night, slowly pushing the last bananas of the day into my mouth, trying to get them all in and hoping they'd stay down. I also used protein weight-gain powders from the health food stores, which I made into milkshakes, five tins of tuna fish a day for more protein, plus the three large meals a day my mother made for me. One thing Al advised me was: never go to bed without having something to eat, even if it was just a cheese sandwich. To a young guy who was trying to gain weight, it was just as easy to come home from working out and go straight to bed. But Al always said, have something to eat first.

So what kept me going along this new path I had forged for myself? I was still quite young when I started training at Al's, but I knew I had to be responsible to be successful. That's why I took my diet so seriously, and I immediately put down the cigarettes I had been smoking to be one of the boys. I had quit playing hockey, so that motivation was gone, and after about nine months I remember a physical fitness instructor from McMaster University asking me "What are you gonna do?" because of the development I was showing. My answer at that point was "Be Mr. Canada." But something else going on at Al's gym was drawing my interest.

Part of the concept of a training facility is being able to watch, train and learn from others. I found myself fascinated by the wrestlers who trained at Al's. The only thing I knew about wrestling up until then was what I used to watch on TV with my grandmother, but here I was, in awe, watching what was going on inside the ring from a front-row seat as I tried to work out. For the first time in my life I saw the wild and crazy physical antics that a person goes through on his way to qualify as a "grunt-and-groan" professional wrestler. During many days, while I would be working out, I'd find myself just sitting and watching, enthralled, 10 feet from two people who seemed to thrive on smashing, crashing and thrashing on each other's bodies.

The wrestlers who trained at Al's gym were mostly local, but other wrestlers would come in off the road to train too because Hamilton was such a mecca for wrestlers. They'd be gone for two or three months, and they'd come back from places like Kansas City or Memphis, and they'd also take a turn in the ring training the younger ones. On Thursday nights Al ran wrestling shows to help support the gym. The gym probably housed about 50 people on wrestling night — they paid a couple of dollars to be entertained. The guys who worked those Thursday nights were mainly the type of wrestlers who keep their day jobs and never go much further than two towns away for shows. Sometimes they'd be on the card wrestling for Frank Tunney when he needed them, at live shows and on the *Maple Leaf Wrestling* TV show too.

It wasn't long after I said I wanted to be Mr. Canada that one of the veterans, a guy named Jack Hill who had taught me a lot about proper weight training methods, said to me, "Come into the ring Dewey, I want to show you some wrestling holds." I had been waiting for a chance like this, so I was quick to respond and got into the ring with him, thinking that I would be finally be learning to body-slam. And I did — but I was on the receiving end every time. I'm sure Jack gave me about a thousand body-slams over the course of these lessons. But I liked it, because he taught me how to fall properly. He also taught me the basic holds: a head lock, hammer lock, top wrist lock and a straight arm bar, plus many others.

Al's gym was also where I had my first *Bang Your Head* experience, so to speak. I had been there about six months and one day I noticed a trapeze hanging from the ceiling, about seven-and-a-half feet up. I decided to make a little display of my acrobatic skills for the rest of the guys and so I jumped up to grab the trapeze bar, and tried to flip my feet over the top to do a loop but misjudged the distance, probably because my legs were too long. Instead I banged my feet on the bar, lost my grip, and fell to the ground, landing right on my forehead. Everyone laughed, and I picked myself up and continued working out like nothing had happened.

Al had to close his gym at King and West and it took the better part of a year before he was back in business. The new wrestling ring wasn't really a ring at all, it was about five layers of 20- by 16-foot pieces of canvas, felt and some carpeting over the old hardwood floor. Wrestling on that surface was like wrestling on solid concrete. Nowadays I can't imagine anyone being thrown on this ever-so-hard and non-giving surface, but we did it all the time. If you wanted to learn, you put up with it. My best move in the ring became the drop kick — a horizontal jump in the air, about five feet, with one foot aimed at the head and the other foot directed at the shoulder or chest area, especially as the opponent is turning around towards you, or has fully risen from getting up from the mat. I practiced drop kicking against the wall too. It's nothing like doing it to another person. If I drop kicked an opponent, he would give, and I would have time to turn. But the wall just — klunk! I got really good at it, and snapping the extension of my legs would create a good jolt. If I could catch opponent with two or three kicks I could usually pin him.

In the meantime another wrestler, Jake Dennet, opened a gym in Westdale beneath a beauty salon, and I started training there. Jake's gym was so small he had to dig the basement deeper in order to be able to stand and press the weights overhead. Jake's expertise and enterprising ways saw his membership grow, and that led him to build a bigger and better gym and combination steam bath on the back end of his dad's five-chair barber shop, still in Westdale and just across the street from his other gym. He called it Contour Health Studios, and it was strictly for bodybuilding, not wrestling. It was a new age gym for those times, and attracted many new members to the world of bodybuilding.

Another strong ambition that began to manifest itself during this period of my life was the desire to travel. I think I caught the travel bug from a boy who lived next door to us when I was about 13. His parents had taken him on a train trip to California, and his tales fascinated me, probably because I had never really gone anywhere besides summer camp. Going on long trips wasn't a thing ordinary people did back then. My love of travel eventually influenced my decision to become a pro wrestler, because it was a career that would allow me to go on the road.

The first trip I took was at age 18, with my old golfing buddy Joe Cheesman. I tend to think of it as a golf tour, because we took our golf clubs with us in Joe's 1951 Chevy and drove through the United States all the way to New Orleans, stopping at different places on the way down to play golf and see the sights. We stopped in Lexington, Kentucky, to see the Man of War Cemetery,

Calumet Farms, the underground caves, and the race tracks, then went on to Little Rock, Arkansas because we wanted to see the school integration that was going on. Being Canadians, we didn't know a lot about the segregation in the American South. I don't want to put a political view on it, because it was something Canadians just heard about, and when we got there and walked around in it, I can't say we got the true feeling of the aggression of the whites and the suppression of the blacks. But as we got further into the South we saw the washrooms and restaurants labeled "black" and "white," and it was all new to us. Still, we decided we would be there for the integration, and we saw the National Guard at the Little Rock high school. It was mostly a tourist's experience; we stayed well back, but we actually witnessed the situation in the Deep South, firsthand.

After Arkansas we headed down to Louisiana. It was probably the state I liked better than any other, because of the friendliness of the people. This was like a foreshadowing of my later career, because I would be in and out of Louisiana many times to wrestle. Joe and I stayed in the downtown YMCA in New Orleans. I was very impressed with the French Quarter. In the daytime people shopped in the fancy stores for luxury furniture and clothing, and then there was the unbelievable nightlife. There were no doors on the buildings because they were open 24 hours. We saw nightclub shows and ate in the fine restaurants there. From New Orleans we crossed over to Florida and drove straight down to Miami Beach, where at that time the black people had to be off the beach at six o'clock. We'd see them lined up on the beach every night waiting to leave.

The next trip I went on was to Miami Beach for two weeks with a couple of friends from Stelco, Tony and Rolly, who also worked out at Contour Health with me. I would call that trip a classic working man's holiday. We stayed at the Sherry-Frontenac Hotel and made the rounds at all the tourist attractions: watching the dog races and jai alai games, touring Cypress Gardens, eating in fine restaurants, seeing the nightclub shows — basically living the high life. We also went to Silver Springs, where they shot the old TV show *Sea Hunt* with Lloyd Bridges, and rode in a glass-bottom boat that let you see right down into the water.

A couple of years later I went on a road trip across Canada with Rusty Davis, my old leader from Camp Wanakita. This was towards the end of my time at Stelco, and I believe I talked Rusty into driving out to Vancouver and hitchhiking back with me — and I say this only because I don't remember Rusty as a very adventurous person. In fact, I admire him for his prudence even today, but I have a feeling that when I showed up back then and proposed the trip to him it might have been a time in his life when he wanted to get away for a while, and that's why he agreed to come with me.

We used the drive-away car system (that is still in place today) to get from Toronto to Calgary, where we dropped the car off. We drove through Northern Ontario: Fort William (Thunder Bay), Fort McCloud, then on to Manitoba, through Winnipeg, Brandon, then followed the Trans-Canada Highway all the way to Calgary. From Calgary we took a bus through the Rockies. We saw the Doukhobors, a small sect of Russian pacifist Christians that live in Western Canada, burning their homes in protest. They lived in the middle of the Rocky Mountains, and I'm not sure exactly what they were protesting, but we saw the fires. We eventually got to Vancouver, and then went on to Victoria to see my cousin Jackie Olmstead and her husband Bruce, who took us out fishing off of Vancouver Island. On the way back we hitchhiked all the way to Hamilton via the United States. It was truly great fun. I wouldn't recommend it now, but back then hitchhiking was quite safe. It was easy to get rides and we met a lot of friendly people.

The last road trip I went on before starting my wrestling career in earnest was with a fellow named John Bell, whom I met at

Contour Health Studios. His father was the principal of Westdale High School. John and I were the same size, probably 200 pounds each, and we had gone into heavier weight training — 300 pounds on the bench press, and I was doing 300 pounds on the squat. I was now 21, had finally quit my job at Stelco, and wasn't sure what I wanted to do with my life. John was out of work too, and I guess I talked him into doing the same thing I did with Rusty, taking a drive-away car out of Toronto for $60 and extra tires, going down through the States via Route 66, then going up the coast of California, dropping the car off in Sacramento and hitchhiking home again.

The trip down wasn't much to talk about. It was a long way down on Route 66, which at that time was the name of a television program. We took Route 66 all the way to Los Angeles, California. We had a very enlightening trip up Highway 1 — that's the one you see in the movies all the time, it runs right beside the Pacific Ocean — and we went straight to San Francisco. We toured San Francisco, Chinatown, uptown, all the things that we wanted to see on our own, and then we headed east to drop the car off in Sacramento. We hitchhiked out of there, stopped in Nevada and spent some time seeing the nightlife of Las Vegas.

It took us 60 rides in total to get from Sacramento back to Hamilton, and for the most part we enjoyed the trip. A lot of memorable things happened along the way. A little boy spilled ice cream all over John while I was sleeping in one car; another fellow had us take over the driving so *he* could sleep; and the woman who drove us from Detroit back into Canada dropped us off in downtown London, Ontario, where it was impossible to get another ride. We had to walk out to the far end of London to keep going.

But there was one bad experience we had that I have never forgotten. It was sometime during the last two weeks of September when we reached Utah, and our driver for that day left us in the mountains above Salt Lake City at a fork in the road. He was going one way and we were supposed to go the other way. We waited but no cars came along, and then it started to snow. I guess it wasn't a blizzard, but it was blowing snow, windy and cold, and all we had on were spring jackets. A couple of hours went by and still no cars had come, and we began to think we might actually freeze to death.

Finally, a young guy about our age stopped and gave us a ride for about 200 miles. I have never forgotten how thankful we were. Just after that came another memorable ride. Two trucks that were caravaning through the mountains each took one of us. They were old vehicles, so noisy that it was hard to carry on a conversation with the driver. My truck had a sleeper bed, which the driver let me use, but the other old truck didn't, and it was so noisy John couldn't sleep, so he had to listen to the driver talking all the time — John said the guy never stopped talking for the whole 32-hour trip. But it got us out of the mountains, and we were grateful for that.

After I got back from California, I got a job near my home in Westdale with George Britton's Furs, and learned how to cut, block and sew furs. Even to this day, I believe that was the best job I ever had. I always liked working with my hands, and the experience came in handy when I created The Missing Link's costume. I also applied for a job with the Burlington Recreation Department, where my friend and road trip buddy Rusty Davis was working. He recommended me and I got a job as the assistant manager at the city arenas, and as a lifeguard at the local pools during the summers.

As you can see, I was never one to just keep doing the same thing for too long. It was the same with my physical training. I continued to train and progress at Contour Health Studios, but I missed wrestling. I found myself back at Al's Gym when he opened a new location in Hamilton, in an old two-storey room with very little heat — the bars sometimes had frost on them until Al got a fire going in the stove. Near the last year of Al's life he was known to have burned anything made of wood that was around the gym, including tables and chairs. By now Al had some new guys training — sometimes pairing off in tag teams, sometimes one-on-one. I fit in well. I learned to take the bruises and bumps, and the proper ways to land and protect yourself, which is absolutely the most important thing a wrestler has to know. Killer Kowalski still tells his wrestling students that. Every time there's a media story on pro wrestling nowadays, they interview Killer Kowalski, and he always says "I tell my members the first thing to do is protect themselves." And you learn not only to protect yourself, but your partners as well. Today's wrestlers are for the most part superior athletes, but the kind of accidents I see happening now tell me that some of them are not being taught the basics of wrestling. It makes me really sad to see talented people sidelined by injuries that are preventable.

So for the next couple of years I was working at my various jobs, working out, and wrestling. It was a rewarding time in my life, since I now had a number of life skills under my belt — I had been active in sports and had a short career in golf already, plus almost ten years in the workforce. Then in the summer of 1963, when I was 24, everything I had been working towards came together so quickly you would have thought I planned it that way.

CHAPTER THREE

Pittsburgh on $25 a Day

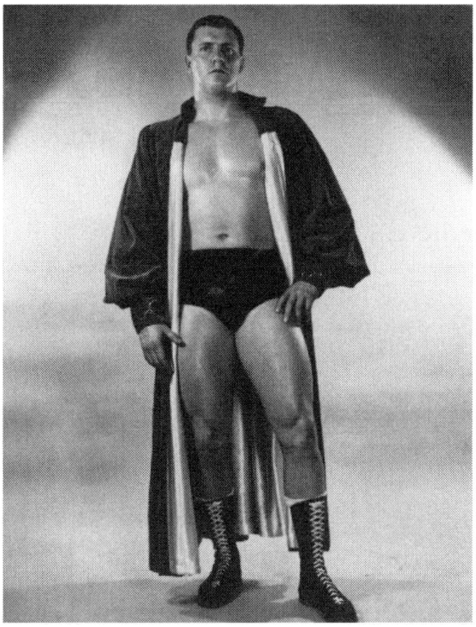

During the time I worked for the Burlington Recreation Department, the city was opening up a lot of public pools, because Lake Ontario was getting too polluted for swimming. There was a group of lifeguards — me, Rusty and some of his water-polo buddies — who would go around to the pool openings and do a little clown act to entertain the people. This was when I started to develop a sense of showmanship. With the confidence and self-esteem I had built up during my weight-training years, a sense of humor and a desire to get people's attention was beginning to emerge in my personality. I wasn't a loud person, but I made sure people knew I was in the room by Missing Link-type antics, even back then. I guess I just wanted to be noticed.

I think we did our clown act three or four times in the period of a couple of years, when they were opening up all these pools, and had a lot of fun doing it. What we did was a combination of a "bucket act" — pretending there was a fire at the pool, and two guys would come running and chase each other around with buckets of "water" that were really just filled with paper — while a couple of other guys did trick dives off the diving boards. At one of the pool openings, I did the trick dives dressed up like a woman. I worked with a woman who was very well-developed. She had a bra and dress that fit me, and I wore very large high-heeled shoes that belonged to her sister. So I ran around the pool in this getup and did my final dive off the high board wearing women's clothes — and landed flat on my back! To this day I still remember how much that stung. Because when you land flat on your back . . . well, I'm sure it was funny to the crowd.

The other memorable show was at the opening of Mountainside Pool, the last one I worked at before starting my wrestling career. I was dressed up in a suit (Rusty Davis claims it was his suit, not mine) and the mayor of Burlington, Owen Mullins, was there with all the town councillors to open the pool. I was one of the attendants that day because people were coming to watch the clown act, and look at the pool and equipment downstairs. I was up on the platform with the mayor to explain the pool's lifeguarding procedures to the crowd. Then the clown act began, and ended up with the mayor pushing me into the pool fully dressed. The photograph of him pushing me into the pool, which showed me suspended in air, made all the newspapers. It was unplanned, but Mayor Mullins picked up on the spirit of the event, and I got my picture in the paper.

One afternoon after Mountainside Pool had been open about three weeks, I was sitting in the office and noticed a pretty, dark-haired, green-eyed girl in a bikini walking around the pool with two young kids. I guess she felt me watching her because she glanced up and I smiled at her, but she kept going towards the shallow end. I waited five minutes, then got up and went over to say hello and ask if the kids were having a good time. She told me the children were her niece and nephew and that she lived with her sister's family across the road from the pool. She didn't seem too impressed with me at first. I learned later that her sister and all the neighbors had been telling her to go over to the pool and meet the head lifeguard (that was me) because she'd just broken up with her boyfriend of three years, but she wasn't in a hurry to meet anyone new. She also thought I "strutted" rather than walked around the pool (which is probably true). But she was back again the next day.

I waited a few minutes while she got herself settled, then went over to talk to her again. I can't say exactly what drew me to her — she was very attractive and had a good figure, but something else told me right away that I liked this girl. She had a bashful and quiet way about her, and I wanted to get to know her. She didn't talk much, and as I got to know her better I noticed she had a slight stammer when she spoke. (I never said anything to her about it, and it eventually went away on its own.) She stayed at the pool for a couple of hours sunning herself and watching me strut around the pool and keep checking to see if she was looking at me. (She noticed right away that I had an ego.) As she got up to leave I popped out of the office to see if she was OK, because she was a little sunburned, and I told her my name. She'd never heard the name Dewey before and thought it was very funny, but I found out her name was Gail.

I didn't see Gail again for almost a week after that, but when she came back again I seized the opportunity to invite her to the pool open house that evening. When she arrived I went over to her right away, took her on the tour of the pool and filter house and kept talking to her afterwards, asking her to a dance the next

Saturday night. She said she was busy but gave me her phone number. I phoned her a couple of times that week and kept asking about Saturday night, and finally she said "Yes." When we got there I introduced her to some friends of mine and one of them, a police officer named Kent Laidlaw, said to her "Oh, you wouldn't go out with me but you would with him, eh?" She had turned him down for a date just before she said yes to me! Everyone had a good laugh about that.

After our first date, Gail started coming to the pool for adult swimming lessons. I found out quickly that she was very afraid of the water, so I took her to a lake on the weekend to gradually teach her how to relax in it. By the time our lessons finished she was able to swim across the pool by herself without being scared. We started seeing a lot of each other, going to parties and dances, and sailing in Toronto with friends of mine who owned sailboats. I always took her home early from our dates because I had to be up for my morning workouts, which she didn't believe at first. She thought I was going out with other girls after I dropped her off.

After a couple of months we were getting quite serious about each other. One night in September we were at a regatta dance and Gail got upset that I was dancing with another girl, so she danced with every guy there but me. By the time the dance was over we were both hurting and angry. Then we found out our plans to stay over with some friends had fallen through so we would have to stay in a motel. Gail was in a panic. She was in love with me but very scared of what might happen if we stayed alone together overnight. It took us so long to find a motel we nearly gave up and drove back home, but finally we found one with a vacant room. I have to admit I used the situation to my advantage. There were two beds in the room but I told her we could only use one or they'd charge us extra.

After we'd both showered we talked about what had happened at the dance, I took her in my arms and told her I loved her, and things took their natural course from there. On Thanksgiving weekend in October I asked Gail to marry me and she said yes. She was 19 and I was 24. I found out years later that the day after our first date she had told a friend of hers at work she was going to marry me. Her friend laughed and asked how she could say that when she barely knew me, but she said she just felt it.

★ ★ ★

When the summer was over, I decided I wanted to try working in sales. Two of my fellow lifeguards, twins Grant and Greg Walker told me about their brother Dean who worked for Underwood-Olivetti, the typewriter manufacturer, and said there was an opening for a salesman in the Hamilton branch. I followed up on the lead immediately and met with the branch manager a few days later. I told him that even if he didn't hire me now, I'd come in to work anyway and they could decide whether I was worth being paid. He gave me the job, and since I enjoyed traveling and meeting people, I moved up quickly. I made extra commissions, they promoted me, and I even got my brother Ken a job in service.

My wrestling career finally got underway right around the same time. While I was still working for George Britton, I had started going to another wrestling school in Al Spittles' original gym. The gym had been reopened by a wrestler named Benny Lima, a smooth wrestling technician who was a former student of Al's. Benny was about 5'8" with a stocky build, and he taught many guys my age one-on-one in the ring.

One day Benny got a call from Bruno Sammartino, who was running the Pittsburgh wrestling territory with the promoter Ace Freeman. Bruno wanted four wrestlers to come down every other Saturday to wrestle live on Channel 11 at 6 p.m. and promote the matches that were run two-and-a-half hours later at the big civic arena. Bruno used a lot of Canadians in the territory and it was a great place for a beginner to break into the business, so of course I jumped at the opportunity — even though I knew I wouldn't be winning any of those matches right away. I would be up against big-name wrestlers who were on the card at the live shows, and my job would be to make the more famous wrestler look as good as possible.

We actually call this *jobbing* in wrestling lingo, and it's always been considered part of paying your dues. It might sound demeaning, but I never thought so. Doing jobs is a very important part of learning the business, because it teaches you how to put the other guy over and make the match look good. And if you do a good job, eventually the promoter will put you in with people who make you look good too, rather than just what we call a *squash job*. This happened to me a lot in the beginning of my career. I was big and muscular and I had a lot of holds. I could take my opponents down and do all kinds of different things. And the other wrestlers didn't mind that, because they knew I was going to be laying my shoulders down for them. I understood the role I was playing very well. The TV shows were set up to provoke people's interest in the main event at the live shows. People in Pittsburgh would turn on the TV while they were eating their dinner and see me being crucified by someone like Big Bill Miller, and say "Wow, I'm going to the matches tonight."

I felt I was ready for it. I was about 220 pounds, I'd been wrestling in exhibition matches at the gym for a while, and I was really looking forward to meeting and learning from veteran wrestlers. And not to brag, but I think my keen interest in learning all I could from the veterans, even when they were pounding the daylights out of me, taking their advice seriously, studying their movements and applying it to my own wrestling, led to my later success. In Pittsburgh I got to wrestle top guys like Big Bill Miller and his very rugged brother, Dan Miller; Gorilla Monsoon; The Maltese Falcon; Dick The Bruiser; Baron Scicluna;

Haystack Calhoun (over 600 pounds!); Chief White Owl; King Curtis (a true gentleman); Killer Kowalski; Professor Toru Tanaka; and many others, including Bruno Sammartino himself.

So this is how my wrestling career officially began: every other Saturday morning at 8:30 I would get in a car with three or sometimes four other wrestlers (and sometimes it was a very small car!) and we would set out for the 325-mile drive to Pittsburgh. I wasn't the sort of person who liked to squeeze into a little car when I was on the road, so when I started buying cars, they were always Cadillacs. I bought my first when I was 18 years old, a yellow 1952 Cadillac convertible. I purchased the rest while on the road wrestling, usually from the southern states where they last longer and are in top shape, but after the many miles I'd wear them out. My thought was always "Well, this is great, I'm traveling and seeing lots of places like I always wanted, so I may as well have a comfortable car." It also meant I could drive other people to the shows and have lots of room for everybody. In the early days there was a lot of budding talent in those cars with me — guys like Big John Quinn, Kurt Von Hess, The Love Brothers and so on. Sometimes there was a lot of fun and camaraderie in the car, but other times it was the so-called *hard way*. In the summertime there was no air conditioning, and in the winter the two-lane highway could get very dangerous, especially through the snowbelt areas where there were lots of trucks to maneuver around.

I bet you're wondering what I got paid for the Pittsburgh jobs. It was $25 a show. After buying gas and food, I'd usually be taking home about $17 for my trouble. I know it doesn't sound like much, but in the 1960s that would pay for several bags of groceries, so it was fair. I never made less than $25 for a match, and I knew guys who started for $8 a show. More important than the money was the fact that I was matched against some very impressive and experienced wrestlers who sometimes made short work of me in the ring. Sometimes it did feel like I was never going to win, but this didn't discourage me. I was developing and improving my ability and performance, and it made me more determined to become a success in wrestling. And I have to say, it was probably feeding my ego.

Something I didn't see until later in my career, when I became a main event wrestler, was how my early experience taught me to adapt my style to accommodate my opponents, who all turned out to be different: short, tall, much heavier than me (300-400 pounds), some with great agility and fast moves, others with bad attitudes. The bottom line was that the hard training I had done was used mainly to keep myself from getting hurt at first — which wasn't always possible, but it could have been much worse for me if I hadn't known what I was doing.

I'll never forget when my turn came to wrestle Gorilla Monsoon. He was larger than life, and I don't just mean in size — though he did weigh over 400 pounds, twice as much as me! The match that night was Gorilla against two opponents, me and Wes Hutchings (Hartford Love). Gorilla was led into the ring on a heavy chain attached to a large dog collar around his neck, and the match began. It was a short one. Wes went in first and Gorilla proceeded to dominate him for about five minutes, finally crushing him with a big splash and throwing him into my corner. I was full of energy and leaped over the top rope, charging at Monsoon and throwing the drop kick that I'd practiced so many times at Al's and Benny's. It was my best move, and it didn't budge Gorilla one inch. I thought "I'll show him," and I jumped again, this time with more impact, my right foot catching the side of his face hard and my left foot high on his chest, with lots of snap in my legs. I might as well have tried to drop kick a mountain. Gorilla just stood there, then picked me up, slammed me and tossed me over into the corner with Wes. His second slam of Wes was followed by two big splashes, then the 1-2-3 count and the match was over. Like I said, some lessons come the hard way, and there would be many others.

Another Saturday I was wrestling Dr. Bill Miller before his championship match with Bruno Sammartino later than evening. Bill, 6'6" and 315 pounds, was a very nice man who would always make the jobber look good so it looked like he was really beating somebody. The match was going well — Bill was lying on his back and I dove on top of him for a pin, but then my hipbone caught him in the eyebrow and, as I was still pretty skinny then, he began to bleed. In those days they had doctors and commissioners onsite who would stop the match immediately if someone got cut, but they decided to let it go on so I never knew the mistake I made. If the match had been stopped it would have made Bill look bad and nobody would have gone to see him wrestle Bruno at the Civic Arena later. But the match was allowed to go on, and all of a sudden I found myself flat on my back and Bill proceeded to paintbrush my stomach with hard stinging strokes. Then he pulled me up, body-slammed me hard, paintbrushed me for the second time and went on to win the match. Another lesson learned the hard way.

I didn't mind the losses. To me it was all part of getting experience, and I had very good experiences in Pittsburgh. Bruno treated everybody well, and as time went on he started booking me in some shows at the Civic Arena and small towns around the territory as well. The territory had been owned by Ace Freeman before Bruno took over, so it had a loose affiliation with the WWWF in New York, which helped me get booked there as well.

★ ★ ★

I was let go from my job with Underwood-Olivetti after only a year, due to a personal misjudgment on my part. I had two machines given to me by a couple of guys who had stolen them — they didn't tell me they were stolen, they just asked me to keep them in my car and I said yes. The funny part about this is

I actually asked a manager about a scenario similar to what these guys were asking me to do, and the manager said not to do it. But I didn't listen. I let these guys lay stolen machines on me and then they got caught. So obviously the machines got recovered when they were caught, and a detective showed up and brought me down to the office to explain my part. I also had to go to a hearing and testify.

This was very traumatic for me. Like I said before, my mother taught me to never tell lies or steal. And I was their top salesman, recently promoted to Special Accounts. Even thought this wasn't really a criminal act on my part — because I didn't really know anything about it, I was just holding the machines — the manager had no alternative but to let me go. I learned a lesson from that. Those guys had tried to use me, and I didn't trust my own judgment enough to say no. But after I found out I could still be held responsible even if I didn't know they were doing something wrong, I certainly never did anything like that again. It reminded me of something that happened when I was 14 years old, and I bet a guy he couldn't eat five 12-inch hot dogs. He ate three, went outside and got sick, came back in and ate two more. I realized I didn't like losing that $2 or whatever it had cost to buy the hot dogs, and I have never bet or gambled on anything in my life since then. I never wanted to feel the way I did when I lost my job with Underwood-Olivetti again either.

I wasn't out of work for long. I immediately saw a job advertised in the newspaper with Office Specialty, an office-furniture manufacturer and supplier. They were going to open a satellite branch in Kitchener-Waterloo and needed a manager. The manager liked me, I got hired and I moved my wife and our new son Mark to Kitchener. We lived three blocks east of the Memorial Auditorium on Weber Street, and my office was in the house, so I was able to work from home for four years. I traveled all over the Golden Triangle sales area: Guelph, Galt, Brantford, Preston, Stratford,

Woodstock and Hanover, helping to design offices and sell Office Specialty furniture. I mention these cities and towns because as my wrestling career grew and we eventually moved out of Kitchener, I went back to wrestle in most of these places many times.

As you can see, things came together for me in an incredibly short period of time. After working hard at a number of different things in my early 20s, I now had a full-time job, a burgeoning wrestling career and a family. I kept increasing my training too. I was still going to Benny Lima's two or three times a week, but I also had access to the local YMCA and the gym in the basement of the extra large home owned by a man named Lloyd Garner. Lloyd was a close friend of Bob Hoffman, who was a famous leader in the world of physical fitness in the '40s, '50s and '60s, especially in the development of weight lifting and proper nutrition products.

The Office Specialty weekly sales meetings were held in Hamilton too, every Monday through the winter, starting at about five o'clock until seven, and afterwards I would go straight to Benny's, then go home. I was notorious for falling asleep at these meetings. Between my job, working out and wrestling on weekends, I needed lots of sleep to maintain my energy level. And sales meetings being, shall we say, not very entertaining, I used them to catch up on my sleep. Anyway, one Monday the branch manager, Bob Shaw, who was also a friend of mine, was waiting for me to fall asleep so he could ask me to demonstrate a particular desk to everybody. Every sales rep would have to do a presentation on some sort of product at the sales meetings. In those days you were expected to have 18 to 20 selling points on a chair or desk. The one he asked me to do was a 60 x 30 metal desk with chrome legs, and there were a lot of points you could bring up, although I can't remember them now. But I wasn't really asleep this time — I'd been waiting for him. When he called my name, I jumped up, ran over, powerlifted the desk over my head and proceeded to demonstrate the desk's selling points for everybody. Well, this broke the meeting right up, and I think Bob Shaw was the one that laughed the most.

This time of my life was very busy, but fulfilling. I started getting more shows in Pittsburgh, some on Friday nights, and some shows after the Saturday TV tapings in a small town outside Pittsburgh. In that case I would stay there a couple of days. I was also doing a lot of local shows on the weekends I didn't go down to Pittsburgh. Eventually I became something of a celebrity around Kitchener. I modeled clothes for a local big and tall men's store and got invited to dinners at the University of Waterloo. I also joined Big Brothers, remembering what it had been like for me not having a father during my teenage years.

One of the less savory aspects of wrestling life I got introduced to early on was the women who liked to hang around wrestlers. There's a disrespectful name for them that I won't use anymore, but suffice to say these women were very much a part of the backstage scene. There's something I want to make very clear to the reader before I go on. Whenever I talk about behind-the-scenes things like the women, and later on alcohol and drugs, or even the politics of who got awarded the belts, I don't want anyone reading this to think I'm pointing fingers or trying to blame other people for my own failings and weaknesses. I'm not trying to pass judgment on anyone's behavior other than my own. Like I said at the beginning of the book, I'm just telling you what happened to me and hoping people will learn from it.

As I remember it, until I was about 17 I wasn't really successful with women. I was never a Don Juan type, sweeping girls off their feet. I was interested in girls but I didn't know how to talk to them, and I was always so busy with my jobs, sports and weight training, I didn't have a lot of time to devote to chasing after women. I had a few girlfriends along the way but never anything really serious until I got married. But now that I was a wrestler, the women were flocking to me with no effort on my part whatsoever, and although I took full advantage of it, I did so with definite feelings of guilt and remorse from the very start.

Out of all the women who attended the shows regularly, there was probably only a handful that hung around the dressing rooms, and they would hang around for many, many years. Sometimes they'd bring in friends, and later on, their daughters. They'd stick around to party, and a lot of them would make themselves available to do wrestlers favors, like picking them up at the airports or driving them to motels, to stay in good standing. Sometimes you could stay over at a girl's house instead of paying for a room — and wrestlers were notorious for finding ways to save money on lodging because promoters never paid for your accommodations. Most of the time one guy would book a hotel room and two or three more would "heel in," so you'd get three or four wrestlers in a room at one cost. So you can see it wouldn't be beyond a wrestler to use a girl's place to stay at (even if her parents lived there too), especially if the payoffs in that area weren't too big.

The promoters themselves always have acknowledged this, and often used it to their advantage. Sometimes they'd even set you up with a girl on your first night in a new territory, someone who'd been around a long time. And if you were going to be in the same territory for a number of weeks or months, you'd develop short-term relationships with women in different cities. This kind of thing went on throughout my entire career.

I knew what I was doing was immoral every time, but it never stopped me. It was just such an effortless, and I have to say, addictive experience, but it *was* morally wrong. I've got to be honest with you. I don't know how others felt about it, but once you cross that line for the first time — it's like a criminal the first time he finds out he can get away with something. He gets addicted to it, and it's that simple. Because the first time leads you to the next time, and as my career heated up, it turned into extremely irresponsible and out-of-control behavior. Nobody thought about safe sex then. The atmosphere was anything goes — different partners, sharing girls — it was all about partying, fame and ego. But whether it was one-night stands or short-term relationships, looking back now I can see it was all a big illusion, just the grass always looking greener on the other side.

I used to take my wife to my matches in the early years, because we were both really excited about me being a wrestler. Most wrestlers didn't bring their wives, and this is why. She would always be sitting in a spot where she could see the dressing rooms and saw very quickly that there were always girls and fans hanging around, desperate with anticipation. She wasn't stupid, she knew it was part of the business and very seldom was I ever asked any questions about where I'd been or who I'd been with. I probably only had to make up stories a half-dozen times in my entire wrestling career. This is inexcusable. In fact, although my wife said early on she didn't care what I did on the road as long as I came home to her, I know now it did bother her very much.

I'll be saying more about how the lifestyle of professional wrestlers affects personal and family life. But there were a lot of positives in the beginning of my career. I'd like to emphasize that. I was able to keep a full-time sales job that let me work out of my house, and still be booked for shows two or three times a week, all within a 90-mile radius. I spent several years going back and forth from Kitchener to Pittsburgh and around the local shows, and my profile got high enough that people began to think I actually was from Kitchener. Then one day I got a call from Frank Tunney of Maple Leaf Wrestling in Toronto.

CHAPTER FOUR

NWA OK

I was elated when I got Frank Tunney's call inviting me to work for Maple Leaf Wrestling. This was a huge step forward for my career. Tunney's promotion was one of the meccas of world-class pro wrestling in the 1960s. When I say meccas, I'm thinking specifically of four cities: Toronto, St. Louis, Houston and New York. Pro wrestling had boomed in Toronto in the post-war period because the chance to wrestle for National Wrestling Alliance (NWA) titles brought wrestlers from all over the world — from countries like Hungary, Japan, the USA, Germany, Greece, Italy, as well as England, Ireland and Scotland — and increased post-war immigration meant that fans of all those nationalities would come out for the shows, from across all the ethnic groups and social classes. It was an exciting time to be a wrestler. I really miss that feeling of a great ethnic mix in the modern era of wrestling. Now it seems like everybody's American with a few Canadians thrown in.

Maple Leaf Gardens hosted up to 20 shows a year, and often the NWA and AWA (American Wrestling Association) World Titles would be defended on the same show. The regulars at Maple Leaf Gardens read like a wrestling hall of fame: Whipper Billy Watson, Lord Athol Layton, Bulldog Brower, Tiger Tasker, The Sheik and Ric Flair. Besides Toronto, the circuit included Kitchener, London, Buffalo, Hamilton and the smaller towns around them.

Frank Tunney was a former president of the NWA, which was founded in 1948 when St. Louis promoter Sam Muchnick and five other promoters from the biggest territories in the American Midwest agreed to promote their shows under the same banner, exchange their top talent, look out for one another against competing promoters, and recognize one world champion. Once they'd agreed on this strategy, the NWA grew into the most powerful and influential governing body in wrestling history. The combined power of the NWA promoters gave them unprecedented control over the sport, allowing them to crush upstart rivals and blacklist any wrestlers who tried to go against them. At its peak, the NWA had 38 members, with offices across the U.S., Canada, Japan, Mexico and the South Pacific, and the NWA World Heavyweight Title became the most coveted belt in pro wrestling. Look at some of the names that have held it: Lou Thesz, Buddy Rogers, Gene Kiniski, The Funk Brothers, Jack Brisco, Harley Race and Ric Flair. I thought if I did well for Frank, one day I might have a shot at that title myself.

So this opportunity was a huge coup for me. I would be a jobber for a while, just like in Pittsburgh, but I would also be wrestling and learning from the best people the sport had to offer. And Kitchener was only about an hour's drive from Toronto, so I could continue living and training there and working at my sales job. Once I began working for Frank, one of the people I began to see regularly was the great Whipper Billy Watson. Even if you're not a wrestling fan you've probably heard of Whipper, and if you are a fan, I don't need to explain how important he was. Besides being one of the greatest wrestlers Canada ever produced (he was World Champion twice), and just as famous for the fundraising work he did with the Ontario Crippled Children's Society/Easter Seals, The Bob Rumball Centre for the Deaf and the Hugh McMillan Rehabilitation Centre, Whipper was also the acknowledged "power behind the throne" at the Toronto promotion. Frank Tunney may have owned the promotion, but Whipper made most of the important decisions.

The first time I met Whipper Watson was at the Hamilton TV station, CHCH Channel 11, where the Toronto office made wrestling tapes that got sold all over the world. He started coming to see me in the Monday night wrestling shows at the Aud in Kitchener, and as I was living close by, I'd bring Frank Tunney and Whipper home to my house afterwards. Anyway, I guess Whipper liked what he saw, because he eventually asked me to become his protégé and tag team partner and to help promote wrestling across Ontario, along with his son Philip. He also offered me a piece of his large rural property in Keswick, a small town about an hour north of Toronto, to build a house on. I accepted his very generous offer, and left my job to become a full-time wrestler. My first week as Whipper Billy Watson's partner I made $8,000 and construction began on a beautiful new home that I designed myself and had built by Whipper's builder. We lived in a rented house in the area for six months while our new house was being built.

The territory Whipper and I were running went west as far as

Chatham, north up to Simcoe County, and as far east as Cornwall. We ran the secondary towns in southern Ontario during the summer, and Frank Tunney ran the big cities. This circuit would keep the Toronto wrestlers who were employed locally for Frank busy when he didn't need them at Maple Leaf Gardens. There were other towns further north run by The Bearman, the late Dave McKigney, who was a thorn in Frank's side until the very end — and that was entirely Frank's doing. Frank hated the idea of competition, and Dave's shows were hugely popular, which rubbed even more salt in that particular wound.

Whipper was very organized, efficient and a man with a lot of wisdom. He was normally quiet when he was around large groups of people, but on the long car trips he and I went on together across our territory, I heard a lot of wise things, and again I have to be honest with you: a lot of it went in one ear and out the other. As I got older, pieces of things Whipper said would come back to me. I remember him telling me, "When the wrestling business is up, it's the best of all. When it's down, it's hard times." It's true — that is wrestling in a nutshell. He was also the first person to tell me the golden rule of publicity: "It doesn't matter what they say about you in the papers, as long as they get your name right."

Whipper Watson's long-range ambition was to take over the Toronto office, but he wasn't going to do it while Frank Tunney was still in charge. But when it was the right time, and Whipper had made all the right connections, he wanted to take the Toronto promotion national, right across Canada. He told me that eventually wrestling would no longer be in cities and small towns, and this tells me that he knew, the same as Vince McMahon Jr., that in the future, television would become the primary medium for watching wrestling. I'm not sure if he knew that the name of it would be pay-per-view, but Whipper Watson was a man of much perspective, and I say this in hindsight because when he first told me that, I didn't believe him. I thought there would always be those small towns — and this lack of insight would come back to haunt me at the end of my career, when what Whipper predicted had changed the nature of pro wrestling and I refused to see it. But Whipper had his plans all laid out and was forging ahead with them, only to have it interrupted by the car accident, hospitalization and then being edged out of wrestling.

But that's jumping ahead. Once Whipper had moved us up to his place and made me his partner, I felt very comfortable working for the Toronto territory, which was large and well-connected. My career was going in the right direction, my family was very happy living in Keswick and I had two sons now — my younger boy Jason had been born while we were still in Kitchener.

* * *

I didn't start out with any outrageous gimmicks in the ring, strange as that may seem for people who only remember me as The Missing Link. Through hard training my body had turned into a natural, symmetrical wrestling body, I had a handle on many holds, and was capable of doing many high spots in a match, but with short hair, my face didn't have much character. And everybody in my life who had watched wrestling would say, "Why don't you get a gimmick, Dewey?" Probably the first person who suggested a gimmick that would have worked was The Bearman. He told me early in my career to let my hair grow and dye it blond, go to New York and Vince McMahon Sr. would probably hire me on the spot, because I would have been a natural replacement for Nature Boy Buddy Rogers. I don't know why I didn't act on his advice, because it was good. I had seen many great wrestling gimmicks along the way — The Spoiler, The Sheik, Kurt Von Hess, George "The Animal" Steele and many more to come — but it wasn't until I finished a heel turn in

Kansas City many years later that I would gain enough confidence to change to a heel gimmick when I created The Missing Link.

Today, I still meet fans from the old days who tell me I was the "all-Canadian" hero to them, so I guess you could call that my early gimmick, but really it was just an extension of my own personality, not a conscious act of any sort. I never got to change my name from Dewey either, which I've always thought was funny because it started out as a nickname I didn't even want, and I used it in Pittsburgh because I wasn't a big star — and then I became a star with it.

There was such a wealth of talent coming through the Toronto territory in the early 1970s. I remember the giant Don Leo Jonathon: 6'6", over 300 pounds, but incredibly cat-like in the ring, with great nip-ups, drop kicks and his amazing flying head scissors. I used to see Don Leo in those TV matches from Chicago that I watched with my grandmother, and then to meet him in the dressing room so many years later, well . . . and when I wrestled him in Hamilton, we changed in the same dressing room that I used to change into my hockey uniform when I was 15. You just never know when great things will happen in your life.

Frank Tunney *married* me to The Assassin in my early years with Maple Leaf — but it's not what you think! In wrestling terminology, being "married" to an opponent means you're booked to wrestle him night after night for a long time. This was very significant for me because The Assassin was really Jack Hill (Jerry Valiant), the man who first introduced me to wrestling eight years previously. He had trained with the best: Buddy Rogers, The Fabulous Kangaroos, Mighty Ursus, Danny Miller, Dick The Bruiser, Ray "The Crippler" Stevens and Pat Patterson, to mention a few. Jack put me through many 45-minute matches (that's what the promoters wanted) and really put a polish on Dewey Robertson's wrestling that helped me later on. He wore a mask as The Assassin, but I could see his grin and hear his chuckly laugh under it as he told me what move to do next. I body-slammed him a lot, and as I had him in the air he would still be whispering the next high spot to me. I get chills when I think about that, because it makes me aware of the focus I had to have in order to be a success in wrestling.

Being picked up by the Toronto office also introduced me to the fine art of wrestling politics, and while being connected to Whipper Watson and Frank Tunney was very helpful, politically, for my career, playing politics was never something I enjoyed. I had become part of a large, successful promotion, and started to see these other people who were always trying to curry favor with the promoters. We called them *office boys* or *stooges*. They were the guys who liked to hang around the office and tell stories on everybody, report to the promoter continually on all the other guys and generally try to get themselves ahead by stepping over other people. Maybe they were trying to compensate for shortcomings in some other area of their careers or they just enjoyed having the promoter's full attention, I don't know. I wasn't interested in playing that game at all.

To me, wrestling was always just hard work, something I enjoyed and something that I wanted to be good at. I got in the ring, enjoyed my punishment, learned the holds, had some great mentors — though there were just as many people who were jealous of me at the beginning. There are always people in any field who resent a new young face, and they didn't mind making things difficult for the new guy. For instance, my gym physique wasn't accepted by everybody. I wasn't the only guy who had some muscles, but muscles weren't a big thing in the post-war era. There were other wrestlers who started out as bodybuilders, but it was more just big, strong strapping men that were the norm. Still, I learned the holds, I learned a lot of things, and I knew wrestling was what I wanted to do with my life. As much as there's a downside to my life story, this was something that was fun.

Being a pro wrestler 35 years ago was very different than it is now. Wrestlers have become mainstream celebrities, like other professional athletes, actors and singers. They star in TV commercials and movies, appear on talk shows to discuss their careers, and strangely enough, people seem to respect their abilities as athletes more now that everybody is more open about what goes on in the wrestling ring being entertainment. When I started I remember people booing, calling us names and saying we were fakes, not real athletes, and the ironclad code of *kayfabe* didn't let us defend ourselves. Kayfabe is a word that comes down from the days when wrestling was part of carnival entertainment, and I don't know what the origin of it is. We also called it *protecting the business*. Keeping kayfabe meant that the promoters wanted to make sure the fans thought everything that went on in the ring was 100% genuine, and they were relentless about it. So if I was wrestling a heel like Reginald Love, who was a good friend of mine, I could not let any of the fans see me laughing or joking with him after the show. We had to pretend we hated each other all the time. And of course nobody could know that it was determined ahead of time who was going to win the matches, although that's what really tested our skills in the ring. We had to put on an exciting athletic performance that looked spontaneous, be aware of the reactions of the crowd at all times, and look like we were hurting each other while trying to protect ourselves at the same time — which was extremely difficult if you had an unskilled or hostile opponent.

I don't know why the promoters were always so paranoid about the fans finding out that the matches were *worked* (predetermined) — but they always referred to the fans as *marks*, which is another carny word that basically means "sucker," and I think that says a lot about the way promoters viewed the fans. When I reflect on that now, maybe it was the promoters and wrestlers who were the real marks, because we thought we were fooling everybody by protecting the business. As far as I can tell, most of the true fans always knew what was really going on and it didn't matter to them. Wrestling was much more than a sport to the fans, it was more like a theatrical presentation with athletic elements — an epic battle between the forces of good and evil where the odds were always stacked against the good guy, just like in real life. Most of the folks who came to watch us regularly were ordinary, hard-working people who didn't have a lot of money and felt that maybe life hadn't been all that fair to them, but for a few dollars they could come out to wrestling and get completely caught up in the drama we created in the ring for them, imagining themselves as the good guy or the bad guy, depending on their own personalities. The lights would go out, the ring would light up, the drama would unfold and they got a chance to holler and scream and let their emotions go without being embarrassed, because everyone else was doing it too. Most of the smarter promoters, like Whipper Watson and Dave McKigney, understood this about the fans too. Vince McMahon may have been the one who finally started calling wrestling "sports entertainment," but I remember Whipper telling schoolkids in the 1960s that wrestling was just entertainment.

★ ★ ★

I didn't have a lot to complain about during the early years of my wrestling career. I was really quite successful. I lived my dream: traveling all over, wrestling all the greats, always learning whatever I could from them and incorporating it into my own wrestling. When I was about 27 or 28, I got to do my first overseas tour in Australia. Frank Tunney made the arrangements and sent me, Tiger Jeet Singh, Don Muraco, and King Curtis from the Toronto office, with Lord Athol Layton as the announcer.

The Australia territory was run by Jim Barnett, formerly of the

Detroit territory. I enjoyed working with Jim very much. He liked me and treated me very well. He was very organized and always paid on time. A typical tour would run about three months and you'd be flying to most of the shows, so Jim made sure that every week you got your plane tickets for that week's matches. He had recently moved into Australia, and they hadn't had American-style wrestling there yet — they were used to amateur-style wrestling, and five-minute rounds — so American pro wrestling really took hold. Jim did terrific business.

It was probably one of the most exciting times in my career. Australia is a beautiful country with beautiful people, exquisite food, and I felt very lucky to get a chance to tour there. I landed there all dressed up in a suit, and it was January the first or second — the middle of the Australian summer — and extremely hot. Fortunately I was able to get a room in a place called the Texas Tavern, which had originally been set up for the guys who were soldiers in the Korean War, so they'd have a place to stay when they were on R&R. It cost me about $20 for a week, it had air conditioning, which is a necessity in Australia, and it was close to the airport. I got to take advantage of some of their outdoor sports while I was there too. I remember doing some scuba diving around some of the reefs they had there, even though the waters around Australia are very dangerous, especially on the Perth side. They have a lot of sharks and stingrays, so you had to watch out in the water. But it was glorious all the same.

There were mostly veteran wrestlers on those Australian tours: Mark Lewin, Wahoo McDaniel, Tex McKenzie, Sweet Daddy Siki, Haystack Calhoun and the like. There were different guys coming in and out all the time of course, that's just who I remember being there when I did my tour. I remember getting along with everybody, and we were all either flying somewhere every day or staying over after a show and flying on somewhere else. Poor Haystack Calhoun used to have a heck of a time getting a taxi to the airport because of his size. In the '70s everyone in North America still drove big cars but all the cars in Australia were what I'd call mid-size, and they'd last a long time because of the dry climate. So these little Greek or Italian taxi drivers would see Haystack, who weighed over 600 pounds, waddling up to the cab with his big bags and take off, because they didn't want him to damage their cars. I'd help out Haystack by carrying both our bags out to wait by the curb for a taxi, then keeping the driver distracted putting the bags in the trunk and talking while Haystack tried to get into the car before the driver saw him. Now, a 600-pound man is going to attract attention pretty well anywhere, and although Haystack would be moving as fast as he could, he didn't always make it in time and would have to chase the cab. He took up the entire back seat once he got in, but more often he'd sit in the front seat. The driver would be squeezed right up against the door and I would sit in the back. He always had to have two seats on the airplanes too. But if we're talking about big wrestlers in cars, I'll never forget the McGuire Twins and their ride. Benny and Billy McGuire together tipped the scales at over 1,300 pounds, and the only way they could fit into a car was to take out the front seat, move the back seat a little bit forward, and add blocks to the brake and gas pedals so they could reach them, the same as the midgets used to do. They also had to be lifted into the ring by machines or "rolled" into the ring by other wrestlers because they were too heavy to lift themselves up onto the apron.

But getting back to my tour of Australia, I started in Sydney, went across the country to Perth, Brisbane and Tasmania, and spent a couple of weeks in New Zealand at the end of the tour. There were local wrestlers on the cards too — Greeks, Italians and other local guys — but the main events were geared around the Canadian and American wrestlers. There was another Canadian who was a very famous wrestler in Australia, Earl

McCready, so as a fellow Canadian too they gave me a lot of good write-ups. A lot of guys went back to Australia many times, because it was such a great place to wrestle. Jim Barnett had his pick of first-rate names to choose from. A number of different territories in the United States were running very well at that time, and he paid top dollar. The fans in Australia were great too. Because even though most of them had never seen North American-style wrestling, Australia is a very sports-oriented country, so they loved the athleticism of it. As I said earlier, North American wrestling fans tend to see wrestling as not only a sport, but also a dramatization of certain basic ideals — good versus evil, fairness versus unfairness, almost as a form of theater — while for the Australian fans, the sporting aspect came first. They cheered for everybody. No matter which dressing room you came out of, they didn't throw things, they didn't treat wrestlers badly and they had a great respect for our abilities as athletes.

★ ★ ★

Right from the start I was considered a serious contender for the NWA World Heavyweight Championship, the belt of belts. Whipper Watson of course had been the World Champion twice, and I think he saw the same potential in me, so very early on he and Frank sent me to Sam Muchnick's territory in St. Louis to qualify. I did my best, but it didn't happen for me. I've always believed it came down to me being too green at the time, and even though I won a number of other prestigious belts, including the NWA Canadian Heavyweight Championship in 1979, I never did get another World Title shot, and over time it became a great source of bitterness for me.

I let not winning that belt eat at me a long time — too long. It wasn't until much later that I realized my role model was Johnny Valentine, God rest his soul, and he never got to be the

World Heavyweight Champion either. And that didn't mean he wasn't good — he was one of the best. Not to put myself in the same class as him, but I was like him in the sense that we could go out and if we had to make the other guy look good, we knew how to make ourselves look good too, whereas the promoter usually wanted the other guy to look that much better. There were probably many wrestlers like me, who had the talent and the ability to become World Champion but weren't considered docile or cooperative enough. If you're the World Champion, you have to do exactly what the promoter wants. Johnny Valentine was my hero, and there were many like Johnny Valentine who never got to be the World Champion because the promoter couldn't depend on them. I always did what I was told, but I wasn't the easiest person to control, and that quality became more pronounced as my career advanced.

★ ★ ★

In November of 1971 Whipper Watson had the terrible accident that eventually cost him the use of his legs. I was devastated, especially since he had been picking up a fireplace screen for my house when it happened. He was standing at the back of his car putting the screen into the trunk, and another car slid right into him, crushing both his legs between the bumpers. He continued to help me with my career, but his own ended after the accident.

In early 1972 a call came to the Toronto office from Leroy McGuirk's Tri-State territory down in Oklahoma. They had The Hollywood Blondes (Jerry Brown and Dale "Buddy" Roberts) as tag team champions, and were looking for a couple of good babyfaces to challenge them for the NWA United States Tag Team Title. So I came down from Toronto and Dennis Stamp came in from the American Wrestling Association (AWA), Verne Gagne's territory in Minneapolis. He and I really clicked as a tag team.

Dennis was a superb athlete, always cheerful to be around, 100% confident and I learned a lot from him. Nobody could control a match the way Dennis Stamp did, and I always knew I could count on him for anything in the ring. The pinnacle of our feud with The Blondes was a match in New Orleans that lasted an hour-and-a-half and ended in a draw. That was the longest match I ever fought. No falls whatsoever in a total of 90 minutes — the action went nonstop and the fans never stopped reacting — which is very unusual for such a long match. Try to imagine anyone doing that now. In Tri-State I also met a lot of people who ended up being very significant to me later on when I became The Missing Link: guys like Ken Mantell, Skandor Akbar, Buddy Roberts, and of course Cowboy Bill Watts, who eventually took over the promotion from McGuirk and turned it into Mid-South Wrestling in 1979.

Dennis and I continued to tag into July of 1973, and then I started thinking about going home again. I had brought my family down south with me. We were living in an apartment in Shreveport, Louisiana, and while I was doing well in Tri-State and probably could have stayed a lot longer, something made me want to return to Canada. I guess I was just homesick. We moved back to Burlington, very close to Hamilton, in the fall, and settled in for the next seven years (the longest we ever lived in one place!).

When I got back from Louisiana, the Toronto territory wasn't doing very well. I would wrestle maybe three days one week, two the next week, then not at all for a couple of weeks. So when a friend of mine suggested, "Why don't you open a gym?" I thought that was a great idea and got right to work. There are all kinds of gyms open now, but in the early 1970s there were very few. I was ten years ahead of the fitness boom, which began after U.S. President Ronald Reagan started telling people to get fit in 1983. It was another type of learning experience starting my own business — always having to be alert and on the ball, and staying optimistic when other people questioned my judgment and asking myself things like: did I really know what I was getting into? I figured that since I had been training in gyms for 15 years, I already had plenty of experience and felt confident that I would have no problems running my own.

I found a 2,000-square-foot space to rent on the second floor of an old warehouse on Plains Road in Burlington and I had about $1,200 saved out of my wrestling earnings to pay for renovations. Even so, much of the work was done on the "barter" system. I had an electrician come in to take care of all the lights and take the ceiling out and hired a contractor to build the shower and dressing room, and I paid them with lifetime memberships instead of cash. I bought a five-foot high wrestling ring in Guelph for $1,500, and a friend who was a welder help me put it together. We set it up about two feet off the ground right in the center of the gym and arranged the weights around it, just the way it had been at Al Spittles'.

Finding equipment was the easy part. I already had a lot of weight-training equipment in my basement, and I had a lot donated to me as well, because I knew plenty of people who had old weights and exercise equipment in their basement they had bought with good intentions but weren't using. People didn't expect the kind of sophisticated machines you see in gyms now, they just wanted a place to lift free weights, a few cable machines you could attach weights to and someone to guide them. I wanted to make my gym look better than the ones I remembered, so I put a lot of effort into fixing it up. I painted the walls, put up beautiful mirrors, long drapes on the windows and built a shower area with a sauna bath. I put Angelo Mosca's football picture up on the wall too — boy, was he mean-looking. When I see him now he has a nice smile on him, but not in that picture.

I called the gym Dewey Robertson's Athletic Club, and from the start it was packed every night. About 125 a people joined the gym a year, and I think my reputation had a lot to do with it. I was well-known in the community and people who joined wanted to be around me and learn from me. I trained a lot of people in lifting weights, and I was always there to attend the clients personally, because we had a very loyal clientele. The gym was men-only at first, because all gyms were men-only back then. I know it seems strange now, but that's the way it was. Women were not encouraged to work out or weight-train, it was seen as unfeminine. But my instincts told me there might be a market for women, so I designated certain hours for women to use the gym, and quite a few women came out to try it. I got a lot of publicity out of that and I became a local celebrity very quickly. People knew me from my wrestling, I was on TV every week and I knew the editor of a local magazine, so I got a lot of write-ups and he started coming to the gym with his son.

I also began training wrestlers two nights a week after the gym closed. In my first year I trained 12 wrestlers, and as well as being very lucrative for me, working with these young guys gave me more insight into my own wrestling. When you begin teaching a skill to other people, you learn as much as they do and I became a better wrestler for it. Iron Mike Sharpe was one of my protégés, and I also trained the late referee Wayne Cashman. My gym produced a few bodybuilding champions too, like local bodybuilder Mike Watson, who went on to win a couple of Mr. Canada competitions.

Soon things were going so well I decided to start holding wrestling shows in the gym on Friday nights, just like my mentors Al Spittles and Benny Lima had done, and drawing on my experience running small-town shows with Whipper in the '60s. It gave my trainees a chance to try out their skills and provided extra practice for all the Toronto wrestlers — Steve Bolus, Billy Red Lyons, Bob Marcus, Terry Yorkston, and many others — who were still suffering from the dry spell in the territory. When I

My loving mother

Great memories of my grandfather

A pleasant childhood

Me and my first best friend

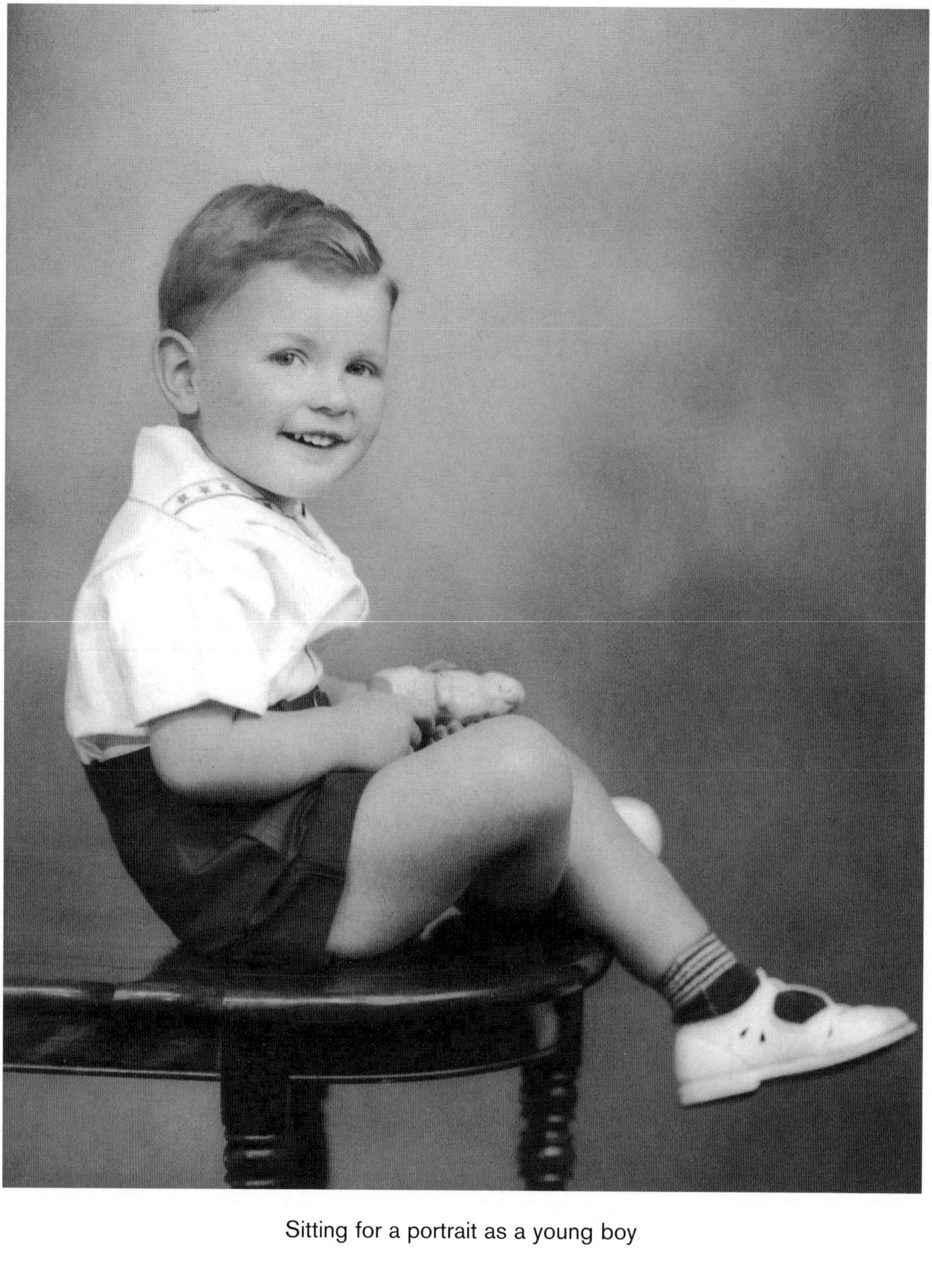

Sitting for a portrait as a young boy

My friend Mike, who's gone, but always in my heart

No trophies, just crests

With the Dundas Grafton's, at 144 pounds

Me, second from left, at a good friend's wedding

My first training partner, Orville Cochran

In Florida, with Tony, at Cyprus Gardens

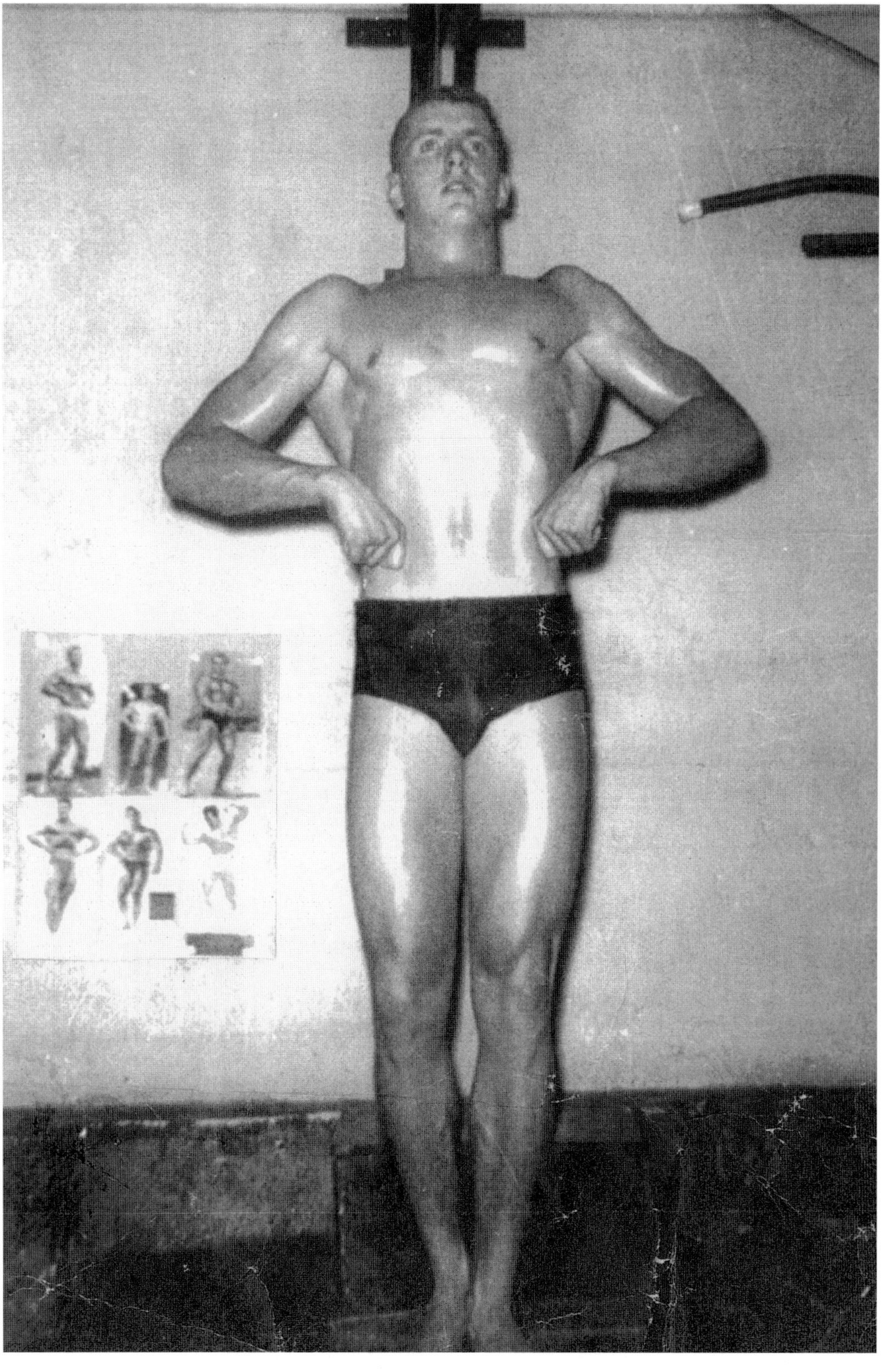

After one year of training, at Jake's Gym

Mid-60s: bodybuilding is paying off

Whipper Billy Watson, Bulldog Brower and Dewey Robertson “wrestling” with my good friend, and the manager of Burlington’s Central Arena, Merv Coleman

"Crusader" Robertson: Toronto success

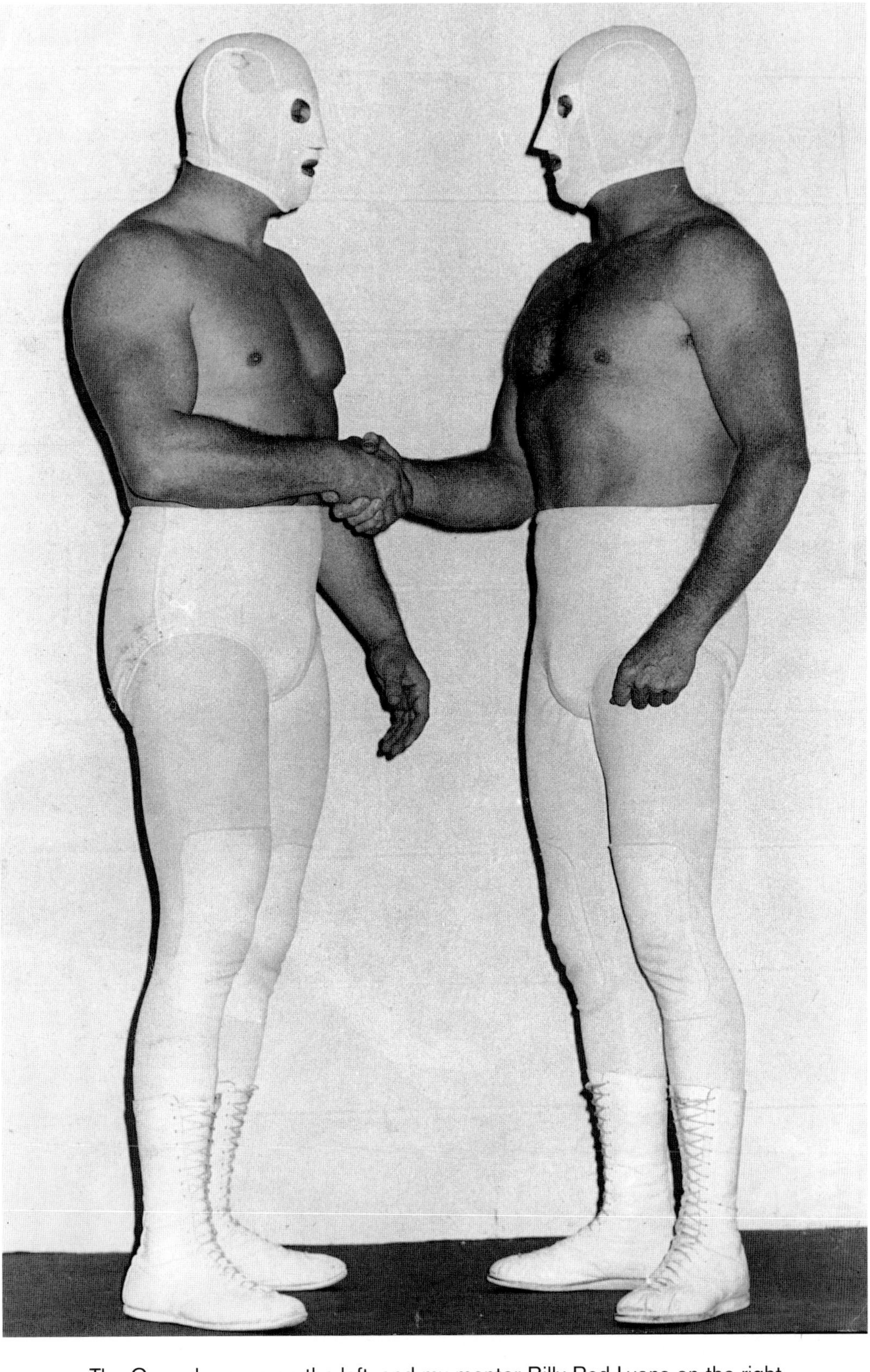

The Crusaders: me on the left, and my mentor Billy Red Lyons on the right

Relaxing at a family gathering

Southern Ontario bodybuilding competition, early '70s

Good times: running my gym in the '70s

Me, the legendary Gordon Solie, and my son Mark Robertson

The beginning of a successful career as a guest speaker

cleared the equipment out and put chairs in, I could squeeze in about 90 people. It was probably beyond the standards of what the building was supposed to hold, but it was a good-size audience for the wrestling. And afterwards I'd host a little party, with some drinks and food, to make it a fun night out for the wrestlers too. A local fan named Kevin Hobbs, who trained at my gym, took pictures and wrote up the results of the matches for the local paper, which meant more publicity.

Running a business was quite an undertaking, but it was a lot of fun and it was the right thing to be doing at that time of my life. It allowed me to spend much-needed time with my family, especially with my wife, who had carried most of the responsibility for taking care of the family when I was wrestling full-time. I got to watch my sons play soccer, lacrosse, hockey — they were a chip off the old block where sports were concerned, that's for sure — take my wife out to the movies and be proud of creating something successful.

CHAPTER FIVE

The Crusader

I tried out my first gimmick after I got back from Tri-State, when the Toronto office was thinking about putting me up against The Sheik. The Sheik was one of the all-time great heels — he could go to main events anywhere in the country, he was so popular. He was the most powerful wrestler, for a long time. I had worked with him before I left Toronto and when I came back, I decided to put a mask on and become The Crusader. My Crusade would be for "clean and scientific wrestling," because The Sheik was one of the dirtiest fighters ever to set foot in the ring — and the fans knew it. The Crusader's outfit was all-white: white boots and tights; white turtleneck and tuxedo jacket; and white mask to contrast against the Sheik's all-black ensembles. John St. John, one of my early wrestling students, played my manager at this time and he wore an all-white outfit too, to provoke a little more interest. Frank Tunney liked it, and after about a year gave me a three match program against The Sheik. Carlos Rocha and a couple of others got to go to five matches, but three was still very good.

If I had known my history better, I might have thought twice about calling myself The Crusader, because the real Crusaders lost their final crusade — and so did I. I had my three matches with The Sheik, lost the third one on April 7, 1974 and had to unmask. I believe the fans already knew who The Crusader really was, but I was doing so well they didn't want me to take the mask off and spoil the mystery. I remember them yelling that: "No, no, don't!" It started with one person, then the whole audience picked it up. But I had to take the mask off and my identity was finally revealed.

Even with the mystery solved, I decided to keep The Crusader gimmick because it was so popular, and began looking for a partner to make it a tag team, so I could go on wrestling solo as Dewey Robertson. I finally teamed up with Billy Red Lyons, which was great. If I had to pick my favorite tag partner, it would probably be Billy. He was a little older than me and had been around longer; he knew every trick there was to know in the ring, and how to keep a match under control. We were also about the same size and weight, and when Billy put the costume on too, you couldn't tell who was who. We used that to great advantage against The Love Brothers, our favorite opponents, when we first took the International Tag Title belts away from them in mid-1974. The Love Brothers were a fantastic heel duo, two long-haired hippies in psychedelic pants and love beads — who weren't peaceful or loving at all — but were both really nice guys outside the ring. Wes Hutchings (Hartford Love) was originally from Newfoundland and moved back East some years ago, but John Evans (Reginald Love) still lives around the Hamilton area and every once in a while we get together to talk about the old days.

The night of that first match for the International Tag Title I went in the ring first, and took 20 minutes or so of punishment, first from Reginald and then from Hartford. They kept taking turns while Billy stood in the corner and watched. The tension and frustration among the fans mounted as I took all the punishment — my partner never came to my aid once. Then Reggie and I crashed head-on into each other and we both fell to the mat at the same time, out cold. Hartford ran to pull his "brother" out so he could take his place and pin me while I was unconscious. But as the referee went over to stop them from pulling a switch, Billy ran over to me, pulled me out, and took my place as the fans went wild. The ref didn't see the switch and since Billy and I looked identical with our masks on, when Billy slowly got to his knees, crawled over and threw himself on top of Reginald for the three-count, the referee was none the wiser. After that win The Crusaders became one of the most exciting tag teams Toronto had ever seen, and for two years running, we were the last match on the card at Maple Leaf Gardens because we provided the most excitement. We defended our title against The Love Brothers, The Kelly Twins, Afa and Sika Anoia (The Wild Samoans), and whoever else tried to oppose us.

I remember one solo match against Reginald Love that ended in an arrest. I had appeared in a TV commercial for a local supermarket chain with Roger Abbott of *Royal Canadian Air Farce* fame — Abbott did the talking while I ripped a phone book in half. A while after those ads ran, I was in the ring with Reggie Love and he started taunting me in front of the crowd, daring me to rip up a phone book and asking for someone in the audience to bring me one. A young man complied with the request, and as I was trying to tear the book the police showed up and took the young guy away for stealing the book from one of the pay phones at Maple Leaf Gardens. Reggie and I both yelled at the cops to leave the guy alone, but it didn't do any good. I can't remember who won the match but I sure remember the phone book!

*   *   *

Life was still treating me very well throughout the mid-1970s. I had the gym bringing in good money, which enabled me to buy a beautiful home with a swimming pool, and my wrestling career still going strong even though the territory was having problems. I did have to take a few breaks from wrestling during this time to deal with severe back pain that turned out to be something called *Ankylosing Spondylitis*, an arthritis of the spine that typically strikes people between the ages of 17 and 35. It's a hereditary condition, nothing to do with my wrestling. AS causes pain and spinal stiffness, and in the worst cases, the spine fuses solidly in a forward-stooped posture. It can also damage other joints such as the hips and shoulders as well as other areas of the body. There's no cure for it but it can be managed if it's caught early enough. Luckily, I was diagnosed early and there was a pill on the market they had been giving to horses, which worked for me as well, so my back's OK — though it does flare up from time to time. It was scary at first, however, because I didn't know that it was coming on, and my back was very bad. I was in a lot of pain and I didn't know what it was until I got to the hospital.

I was also out of commission for about six weeks in 1976 when I broke my leg defending the International Tag Title against The Kelly Twins. The situation was that Mike Kelly had been drinking and made an error. We were off-balance and I couldn't land properly and broke my leg. Fortunately, it happened right at the end of the match, where Red Lyons was right there to tag me, but I mention this incident because it's a perfect illustration of how wrong the notion of pro wrestling being "fake" is. People ask me continually, "Do people get hurt?" as though it couldn't be possible. Somebody once said to me, "Oh well, aren't a lot of these mistakes?" Well, yes they are, but the best way I can illustrate is by telling you a story about one time I was watching my own son Jason wrestling at a Kiwanis park. My boy's a flyer, and he dove off this guy halfway across the ring but as he came down, he hit his left wrist on the mat (instead of landing on the flat part of the forearm like you're supposed to) and knocked his elbow out of the joint so his forearm fell backwards. He rolled over and pulled the forearm back into place, pinned the guy quickly and rolled out of the ring and went to dressing room holding his arm. Another wrestler, my good friend Ricky Johnson (who is Rocky Johnson's brother, and The Rock's uncle) was watching with me and said, "Better him than me!" That sounds callous but any wrestler knows what it means. You want to be careful and protect yourself, but when you're in the heat of battle and bodies are flying around the ring, there are a lot of things you can't control. When Jason came in the dressing room afterwards, Ricky and I were sitting by some mats on the ground. Jason just sat there touching his arm. As he got his breath back and started to relax, he slowly reached up to stretch his arm as though he was feeling better. But as his arm began to stretch to where his shoulder was, the forearm fell out of the elbow socket again. Even now I can't describe my feelings for Jason when that happened. All I can say is: there's a lot of pain in wrestling.

Today, when the fans are so much more knowledgeable about wrestling, people still seem to have the idea that "fake" means "not dangerous." The truth is professional wrestling is a highly skilled sport and the physical danger is real, even if you're really good. Accidents happen, and the rigors of touring and drug and alcohol use all add to the risk factor. The list of injuries that are inflicted upon wrestlers run a huge spectrum, from minor injuries like jammed thumbs, broken wrists and mild concussions to major ones like broken legs, torn cartilage or ligaments and fractured vertebrae. Occasionally, wrestlers are killed. I wrestled several thousand matches between 1961 and 2005, and in addition to getting stitched up too many times to count, pulling a lot of back and groin muscles, pinching many back and neck nerves, tearing ligaments, spraining my ankle and bruising my feet and toes, I have fractured my skull, broken three ribs, shattered my kneecaps and elbows, broken my leg and dislocated my sacroiliac (hip bones). Not one of those injuries was "fake."

And there was no point in looking for sympathy for getting hurt from your peers, because you wouldn't get any. The attitude was always, "It looks good for the business" if you were a promoter or, like Ricky Johnson said, "Better him than me!" if you were a wrestler. Rowdy Roddy Piper summed it up well: "You find sympathy in the dictionary after shit and suicide." Injuries were considered an occupational hazard and no one wanted to listen to anybody's complaints, because all of us were suffering equally. Wrestlers did not always have long careers either. I probably saw several hundred wrestlers not even make it to five years for any number of reasons — everything from injuries, territories not having vacancies on their cards, not having enough personality to interest promoters — and so a lot of these guys ended up never leaving their hometowns and eventually getting day jobs and wrestling part-time, or giving it up entirely. I was very fortunate to have as long a career as I did, especially considering how much I abused my body with alcohol and drugs later on.

The constant risk of injury isn't the only hazard you face in the ring. Pro wrestling is not a sport that generates much in the way of compassion or empathy among its practitioners. Wrestlers by and large are not friendly people. The interaction between two wrestlers in dressing rooms and on the road (whether traveling by car or airplane) might not have any camaraderie but in the ring you're expected to fake it, and do your best to put on the most exciting performance possible. What often happened instead was deep-seated resentments would cause conflicts in the ring, and as a result, the performance would be ruined. Jealousy often develops between main-eventers and the guys further down the card. The main-event wrestler would get insecure because he was always in a precarious position. In the promoter's eyes the main-event wrestler was the guy capable of drawing the most money, even if the guys lower down on the card were better wrestlers or even just harder workers. This insecurity, added to the resentment directed at the main-eventers from the other wrestlers on the card, who would have to put in longer matches for less money (the main event was normally a short match). It created a lot of animosity and pettiness that would sour everybody's attitude.

Performing in the ring also fosters the growth of egos. Big ones. One night you might be in front of a small crowd and the next a stadium crowd of 20,000 to 50,000. But however big the audience was, you were always in the spotlight, with people cheering and reacting to your every move, and that can get addictive. You start to want (and later on need) that kind of adulation all the time, whether you're in the ring or not, and over time this need can get out of hand and create a disruptive personality.

★ ★ ★

Billy and I took the Crusaders to Japan in early 1977. All the NWA promotions were sending wrestlers to Japan and I had always wanted to go. I've been back since, but this was my first time. The promotion was owned by Giant Baba, a former baseball player, who came to Canada to train in physical fitness with Fred Atkins down in Crystal Beach. Fred's basic training included cable weights and running on the beaches to get in shape — he trained Tiger Jeet Singh the same way. There were only three companies in Japan back then, and they all paid very well, like Australia. Bruno Sammartino made so much money wrestling in Japan he bought Giant Baba a brand new Cadillac and had it shipped it over there. It's changed a lot since when I first went over. For a time there were as many as 18 or 20 wrestling promotions in Japan, but now they're back down to about half a dozen, and of those, I think two or three are women-only. The Japanese women wrestlers are extremely good — they're not that big physically, but they give performance plus and a good style of wrestling.

Billy and I went to Japan to defend the International Tag Title, which we had won again in Toronto. Billy had toured Japan once already with his brother-in-law Dick Beyer, The Destroyer, so I appreciated going with someone who knew the ropes. In Japan they have a lot of English signs, but not many people actually speak English. However, the Japanese are extremely friendly and polite. They would always invite us to their homes for a meal, give us a ride if we needed one, carry our bags for us, everything.

Billy and I got there in January, and in Japan, most of the wrestling forums are unheated. The fans would sit cross-legged on the floor and they were always quiet, they didn't cheer or boo or clap or anything. You'd be going into these little tiny villages way back in one of the mountains or wherever, the place would be full, the fans would be sitting on the floor in the cold and we'd be sitting in the dressing room with our wrestling gear on and our heavy coats over it to keep warm. We took our all-white costumes with us, and we also wore a split Olympic-style costume that was red with white piping and our white masks with the letter 'C' on the back for some of the matches.

One thing that caught my interest in Japan was the sumo tournaments. They were into the finals, I guess you'd call it, while we were there, and in Tokyo I noticed these poles in the dressing room: about eight feet tall, and almost a foot thick made out of some kind of incredibly smooth and hard wood. Maybe bamboo or teak, I wasn't sure. These poles were for the sumo wrestlers to practice on. Huge 300-400 pound men would push on this thing to build their shoulder muscles because sumo is a pushing sport, all about trying to knock your opponent off balance. When I leaned my shoulders on it I found it was very uncomfortable and I wasn't even pushing. I figured they must have to do some kind of squats or leg work too, to build up those muscles, and of course they're always eating, to build up to such size. It was a different way of training than the one I was used to, and it impressed me.

Another exciting thing happened during the summer the Canadian National Exhibition was celebrating its 100th anniversary. They wanted to put on wrestling shows like the ones back in the 1920s, when wrestling was part of the carnival shows. Back then all the carnivals would have at least one big guy, and sometimes women too, who would challenge the locals to a wrestling match for money. There would always be a few big farmers and brawlers in the audience (who were often planted by the carnival barker) who would take up the challenge and entertain everybody. They wanted four wrestlers to work 17 days straight, every half hour from noon to midnight — I worked out a schedule and most of the details myself with the guy from Conklin Shows. They hired actors from Toronto to be barkers and they blew their voices out in days. I played the booker and called myself Big Lou Clayborn, a character modeled on a real Hamilton booker from the 1920s, John Katan. We also planted shills in the audience just like the old days, too, because we couldn't take a chance on nobody coming up for the challenge. It was a lot of fun. People dressed up in 1920s clothes, it only cost 25 cents to get in, and my wrestlers got $500 each for 17 days work.

* * *

While I ran my gym I laid plans out for a newer, bigger operation, because after three years in business I had made so much money I was able to buy my own building. I don't know why that was so important to me — I had it made at the site I was at already. I guess I wanted to build a more up-to-date weight-training facility. The new site was on the Kingsway Road near the Guelph Line and had been a catering kitchen previously, so I had to get a crew of nine young men to come in and help me tear down the two big freezers that had served 19 restaurants in the area. Within five weeks I'd ripped it all out, started moving the sauna over, put in a beautiful gold carpet, had a design person from the newspaper show me how to paint the walls white with a nice stripe and put in new, up-to-date equipment. I didn't take the wrestling ring with me because I was just going to start with bodybuilding and had plans for adding on later. Not taking the ring turned out to be a mistake.

I called the new place Dewey's Gym, and replaced my old yellow van that had lots of advertising on it with a new bright orange one with *Dewey's Gym* airbrushed on it. I drove a lot of wrestlers back and forth from matches in that van. André The Giant was one of my regular passengers. I had first met André in Kingston, Ontario, when he was working for Johnny Rougeau in Montreal, then I saw a lot of him when he was wrestling in Toronto. He liked riding in my van because he could sit on the floor in the back and stretch his legs out all the way. His head would almost cover the whole rear window and block me from seeing out the rearview mirror. André's hands were twice the width of my large hands, and the Western boots that he always wore were size 22.

It was lucky for me that André The Giant was truly a gentle giant, because the first time he was invited into Frank Tunney's office, he got subjected to Frank's favorite rib for new wrestlers and I was the one picked to flip the switch. In most wrestling territories there were standing *ribs*, or jokes, that were regularly pulled on newcomers, and Frank's rib involved a chair in his office that was rigged up to a light switch on the wall.

I was already in Frank's office when André arrived, sitting on a chair near the switch. I was unaware that I was told to sit there purposely. André was told to sit on another wooden chair about 10 feet opposite me, and then someone's voice told me to flip on the light switch. I didn't know it but this was the switch that turned on 110 volts of electric power that ran to the seat of the chair that André was sitting in. That was enough juice to give an ordinary man a good jolt — I remember doing it to Big Tex McKenzie another time, and he shot straight up, long arms and legs flying all over the place. But in André's case, the expression on his face showed his surprise, then he stood up very slowly — all 7'2" and 400-plus pounds of him — and rubbed the seat of the chair thoughtfully, all the while looking directly at me with my hand still on the switch. He took about three steps towards me, cracked a huge smile and reached out to shake my hand. Then my heartbeat went back to normal and I realized everything was OK. Praise the Lord.

Going out to dinner with André was an experience too. He'd always order double of whatever I ordered: two steaks, two orders of potatoes, two salads, a dozen slices of bread, and two slices of apple pie à la mode, and get really grumpy with the wait staff if they didn't understand him. However, for sheer appetite, no one could match The Beast (Hamilton's John Yachetti). He could eat more at one sitting than André or Haystack Calhoun. There weren't a lot of all-you-can-eat buffets back in the 1970s, but no matter where we were on the road, The Beast could sniff them out like a dog after a bone. The owners got to know him after a while and would shudder when they saw him coming in, because they knew they'd be losing money that evening. I usually made about four visits to the buffet table then I would have to sit, squirming with embarrassment, while The Beast made a fifth, sixth, and seventh trip. The other patrons, wait staff and cooks would all be watching too, and I sometimes wondered if they were taking bets back in the kitchen. One time a fan came up to our table after The Beast had finished his seventh plateful of food and bet $20 that he couldn't eat six Hershey's bars in 20 seconds. I guess the guy figured that even if The Beast could possibly still be hungry, it would be physically impossible to eat that much chocolate in such a short time and he'd make an easy $20 and have a good story to tell.

The Beast had no worries. He happily accepted the bet and the Hershey's bars. He unwrapped the bars, stacked them one on top of each other, said to the fan, "You have a watch?" and he was off. The Beast bit through the stack of bars as easily as if they were a peanut butter sandwich, chewing each huge hunk of chocolate just a couple of times before taking another bite. He finished with a big smile on his face and about 15 seconds to spare. He pocketed the money, and as we got up to leave he shook the fan's hand and said, "Thanks for the $20 and the six chocolate bars, I'm almost full now."

CHAPTER SIX

Canadian Heavyweight Champion

In 1978, the Toronto office got into financial trouble and the territory was slumping again. The AWA tried coming in for a while to bring it up, but that didn't work, then Frank Tunney and Jim Crockett got together. Jim was running NWA Mid-Atlantic Championship Wrestling out of Charlotte, North Carolina, and that territory was doing very well, so Frank ended up selling a chunk of Maple Leaf to Jim Crockett. Another piece went to his booker, Hamilton's George Scott. Frank stayed on in Toronto, but Jim Crockett was the one running the show.

When Charlotte came to Toronto I was still one of Toronto's fixtures, because of my association with Whipper Watson. Once the Charlotte wrestlers were coming in and out regularly, the territory picked up again. Former World Tag Team Champion George Scott, who was originally from Hamilton, was the booker for Mid-Atlantic and he invited me down to start wrestling in the Charlotte territory. George always looked out for other Hamilton guys. I wasn't figured in to be a top guy, but Charlotte was running three successful shows per night along the East Coast all the way from Virginia to lower Georgia so there'd be lots of work, and the payoffs were anywhere from $800 to $1,500 a week, which was very good money.

I wasn't pressed for money right then. Even though the Toronto territory had been stagnant for most of the '70s, I had a good income from the gyms and my main-event run as The Crusader, plus a big house on a double lot that could be sold later if I needed more cash. I probably would have managed just fine if I'd stayed in Canada but I was always on the lookout for new and better opportunities, so I made the decision to pack up my new Ford van and drive it down to North Carolina.

I checked into the Days Inn outside Charlotte where all the Mid-Atlantic wrestlers stayed when they were in town for a show. I wrestled in Charlotte that night, went back to my hotel room after the show, but instead of going to sleep I packed my bag and started driving north again (without telling George where I was going), calling my wife from somewhere near Pittsburgh to say I was coming home. She was surprised, as she had already thrown a big going-away party for me when I left. I explained to her that I liked Charlotte — it was a beautiful city, a good territory, and I knew I could make a lot of money there, but I'd made up my mind I wanted my family there with me. Being a wrestler is rough on family life — having to go on the road for months or years at a time, the isolation, the loneliness, and the responsibilities always falling on the spouse who stays home. Basically there's two things you can do: leave your family behind when you go on the road and try to get home as much as you can, or take them along with you. I did not like being separated from my family for long periods of time, so I told my wife I wanted her and the boys to come south and live there too. Once that decision was made I finally thought to call George Scott from Canada and told him I was home packing to move everybody down to Charlotte. He was very relieved to hear from me, as they had been calling all the hospitals and had the police out looking for me for two days because nobody had any idea where I was. He was glad to hear I was planning to come back. Poor George. That was only the first of many sleepless nights I caused him. I really owe him an apology for all the stress I put him through when we worked together.

My wife and I asked some friends to rent out our house in Burlington and made arrangements for people to manage Dewey's Gym for us, and everybody came down to North Carolina with me. At the time it never occurred to me that taking the whole family down to Charlotte was a selfish thing to do. My family had always supported my career, so I didn't even think about what I was asking them to give up just because I was lonely down there. We had a beautiful home with a pool in the backyard, three vehicles including a truck, my wife had a good job and both my sons were triple A hockey players, already being scouted in Canada when we moved. Charlotte had one not-very-good hockey league and the practice ice was in a mall where they had public skating. However, Charlotte was also an incredibly beautiful city, with warm weather and friendly people. In fact, the whole of North and South Carolina is beautiful, even though when you get to the coast you're in the hurricane area. The Mid-Atlantic territory covered most of the major cities in North and South Carolina and Virginia: Winston-Salem, Charlotte, Greensboro, Raleigh, Asheville and Fayetteville; Charleston, Greenville, Columbia and Spartanburg; Roanoke, Norfolk, Richmond and Hampton.

There was a wealth of top talent in Mid-Atlantic when I was

there: Blackjack Mulligan; Rocky Johnson (The Rock's dad); Greg Valentine (Johnny's son); The Youngbloods; Dusty Rhodes; John Studd; Ray Stevens; Ricky Steamboat; Dory Funk Jr.; Baron Von Raschke and Ivan Koloff, who was one of the best. When I was training with Al Spittles, Ivan was at Jake Wentworth's, and as The Russian Bear he quickly became a main eventer everywhere (he was from near Ottawa and really French Canadian) — Vancouver, Montreal, New York, Toronto — and found his niche in Charlotte. It was Ivan who finally took the WWWF Heavyweight Title from Bruno Sammartino in 1971, after Bruno had held it for nearly eight years. I only had the honor of wrestling Ivan once, in Montreal. Who else was there? Jimmy Superfly Snuka, another former bodybuilder and probably the wrestler who made all the others most aware of the importance of having a gym physique. Jimmy was an eight-time Mr. Hawaii and had been a cliff diver for the tourists too. And of course, Rowdy Roddy Piper, who became a good friend of mine. Roddy had a lot of people convinced he was a real Scotsman but he was actually Canadian, a prairie boy from Saskatchewan — what more can I say? There was always a special bond when you met a fellow Canadian on the road, and there were plenty of us to be found in the U.S. regional promotions. A wise Canadian will acknowledge that it's a good feeling to know that the USA — the most powerful nation on earth — considers us its younger and smaller brother, as my mentor Whipper Watson always used to tell me.

Roddy became nationally famous when he joined the expanding WWF, but my personal feelings about Mr. Piper, as Vince McMahon would call him, was that he should have been chosen to be NWA World Champion, because he had all the qualifications. A great talker and superb performer in the ring, he could draw the fans out everywhere, from small towns to big-city stadiums. However, he ended up doing very well for himself in the WWF and I was happy for him, because he deserved it. Roddy was always very focused on his career, but he didn't ever imagine he'd make the kind of money that he'd be getting in New York in a few years. What I remember from dressing room talk was that all he really wanted was enough money to buy a farm to live on with his family, which I believe he has accomplished. Roddy always gave 100% when he was in the ring, and I can remember him practicing his interviews before matches, which paid off for him later on when he did Piper's Pit in the WWF and interviewed other wrestlers. One of my career regrets is that I never got to wrestle him after my transformation into The Missing Link. And last but certainly not least, there was the undisputed leader of the Charlotte pack, Nature Boy Ric Flair, master of the figure-four leg lock, just starting his incredible main event run. When this crew started coming to Toronto, the fans went wild, and all of us benefited from the boost in popularity.

Going down to the Carolinas was a great move for me career-wise, but unfortunately, it was also where I began mapping out the path for my eventual downfall. To put it simply, I fell into the syndrome of the wrestler on the road. Before moving to Charlotte I'd had the responsibility of running my own business to keep me on track, plus I had a lifestyle that was very family-oriented and stable. But society was changing then and wrestling along with it. At the time I arrived in Charlotte, a new generation of wrestlers was coming to prominence and there was a much wilder party scene than anything I had experienced. There was a lot of drinking and a lot of drugs.

The drug scene was completely new to me. I didn't do any drugs or even drink alcohol to a great extent when I was young because I'd always been so careful about my health. So I was very healthy at that age, my late 30s, and I'd maintained working out in the gym almost every day. But now there was a lot of peer pressure to be one of the boys, and gradually I gave into it. First I abandoned my previous two-to-three beer ration and started drinking as many as I could hold. I probably never drank more than ten beers at one sitting, because whether you're partying in the car or a hotel, it's hard to drink a lot of beer. But I was also getting into hard liquors and wine too, mixing everything up. So I'd usually start the night off with beer, move on to whisky — Seagram's and Canadian Club were my favorites — and finish off the evening with cheap wine or Thunderbird. I used to take Thunderbird to parties with me to pour a drink for everybody and they didn't know what they were drinking. That's probably a good thing — it's raunchy stuff.

Around the same time I was introduced to marijuana and it became my drug of choice from that moment on. I smoked it constantly, from early morning to late at night, for the next ten years. People think marijuana is a "soft" drug that isn't as harmful as the others, but I'm telling you: ask me to my face, like Mosca used to say, and I'll tell you about marijuana. Marijuana's been a thorn in my side for a very long time. I'm 16 years sober now, but probably only ten years clean from marijuana, because when I'm feeling down that's the addiction that comes back to me. People think marijuana's a drug that won't hurt you, but any addiction, whether it's to a substance, like alcohol or marijuana, or a behavior, like gambling, can come back to you at any time. I've seen people stay sober for 30 years and all of a sudden they start to drink again. Nobody knows why. Nobody tells you about what happens, how many suicides occur or how many people die at young ages because of alcohol and drugs. *TIME Magazine* published a story awhile back about marijuana, citing several studies that show some people do get addicted to it. Heavy users can experience withdrawal symptoms like anxiety, trouble sleeping, and stomach pain when they quit. They also estimate that about 9% of marijuana users develop a dependence, which may be low compared to alcohol (15%), heroin (23%) and cigarettes (33%), but I can tell you right from my own experience that it's true.

My marijuana use started off slowly at first, because I didn't really want the promoters to know what I was doing. You'd think that would have tipped me off that it was wrong, but it didn't. And I was warned at the very beginning by George Scott, who saw what I was doing and cared enough to take me aside and tell me gently that this was the wrong direction to go in. He called me into the office one day — I sat down and he stood up like a gentleman and gave me a short lecture on marijuana that I didn't listen to, because I was enjoying some success in the new territory and it was feeding my ego. Don't think for a minute that teenagers are the only ones vulnerable to peer pressure because they're inexperienced. Here I was, a veteran with a decade-and-a-half of experience under my belt. I was with a bunch of new guys who were 10 to 15 years younger than me and you'd think I would know better than to let *them* influence *my* behavior. But no, I was enjoying being a star too much, and I wanted to be one of the boys, so I jumped into the partying with both feet.

There were other, harder drugs around the scene too: mostly cocaine, speed and pills, but I never got much into any of those. I have found out in the course of my rehab and therapy that I am a manic-depressive or bipolar personality, which means I have highs and lows, and that's probably the reason I never got hooked on cocaine. I hated the "speedy" feeling you got from it. It made me feel too out of control. A lot of people took pills too, to calm down after matches: Valium, Tuinal, Seconal, Quaaludes, Placidyl, Tylenol with Codeine, and probably others I don't know the names of. The pill world is a whole different world — I've heard of people who take Valium for 20 years at a time, and I'm just lucky I never got into that heavily either. I never liked taking pills.

The other drugs I started using regularly around the same time as marijuana were anabolic steroids. To be fair, in 1978 people didn't know yet how dangerous they were. You could go to a doctor and get a prescription for them, no controversy, and there was a "grapevine" that let you know which doctors were best to go to. Steroids had been available in a pill form since the 1960s: you could get 100 Dianabol pills for $25, and some guys would be taking a bottle a day. There was a thriving black market too, where the stuff went for more than double the prescription rate. When I started taking steroids it was by injection, and I always stayed on "the program": two ccs of injectable testosterone, one shot a week, 21 days on, 21 days off.

You might well ask why I took steroids at all, because I didn't really need them. I was already 245 pounds, with a good physique. But people kept telling me I had to try this stuff to keep up with everyone else, and I succumbed to peer pressure again. Steroids didn't make a huge difference in my body — I got a little stronger, a little more cut, my muscles felt bigger and harder and I could take more punishment in the ring. I didn't know yet about the long-term internal damage they were doing. The increased risk of heart attack from elevated blood pressure and cholesterol levels, the strain on the kidneys and liver, the impotence and sterility — that was still to come.

But even with all that, the worst damage steroids did was inside my head. Steroids are hormones, and they throw your moods all out of whack. When I started using steroids I experienced an immediate personality change. Suddenly I was always anxious and on edge, and I had been a very easygoing type of person previously. Then when the anxiety wore off, depression would take its place. This cycle of destructive moods gradually entrenched itself in my personality. I was able to manage the mood swings at first because I was still very happy at what I was doing, and I had the discipline of 20 years of bodybuilding behind me. I still worked out very hard in the gym, pushed a lot of weights, and that probably relieved a lot of the worst effects of steroids and drugs, or I wouldn't have been able to carry on as long as I did. There's quite a few guys my age or younger who aren't with us anymore because of the way they abused their bodies with steroids, alcohol and drugs. But that constant feeling of tension and anxiety from the steroids was horrible. Anxiety is a very difficult thing to deal with, and if you don't get to the gym and work it off, that tension you feel in your body will come out as aggression, or what they call "roid rage" now. It was especially bad for the younger guys, the ones that were counting on the steroids to give them a body, mixing them up and taking too much at once. They didn't understand how the stuff would affect them. They wouldn't see the mood swings coming on, and then out of nowhere they'd "pop" — go into a sudden rage over something really minor and lash out at whoever was closest. When you're wrestling full-time you have a lot of anxieties anyway, about your position on the card, how much money you're getting and who you have to wrestle, and when you throw steroids into that mindset, things can get explosive.

I well remember the tension of sitting there and having to take it, but I didn't lash out at anybody, never talked back to promoters or picked on other wrestlers. But there were other guys who couldn't contain themselves, and a lot of guys would end up taking painkillers or tranquilizers to settle their nerves. I never did. I just didn't like the idea of taking pills. This doesn't mean I was any better than they were, and in fact most people would think my way of dealing with it was worse. I held in the rage until I got home and then I'd take it all out on my wife. I'm ashamed to say it, but that's the truth. No sooner would I get in the door then all the anger and tension I'd been holding back would cut loose and I'd blame her for everything I was unhappy about. This got worse as time went on. She became a hostage to my rages and disgusting, addiction-fueled behavior and I am deeply, deeply sorry for what I did to her.

It wasn't just the steroids that were bringing out the anger in me. When I look back now, even with the hard time I've had trying to stay off marijuana, I really think alcohol was the worst thing for me. My father had been an alcoholic, but I had always been such a light drinker, I thought I had that licked. Yet once I started drinking heavily, I found out alcohol has a way of bringing out tendencies and driving forces in you that you never knew were there. Abusiveness, promiscuity, egomania, bad judgment, impulsiveness, you name it. My wife was a classic co-dependent caretaker-personality too — they're the type who can't say "No," however badly the addict treats them, and because of that they end up becoming a partner in the addiction and increasing their own suffering. It was a gradual process, though. At the beginning I was happy in Charlotte, and she liked it there too, and it just seemed like good times and partying, to celebrate my success in the new territory.

* * *

Towards the end of 1978, there was some trouble back home in Canada with the gym. I sent my wife and sons back to Burlington two weeks before Christmas to see if they could fix the situation, and I got there just after the holidays. I kept going back and forth from Charlotte to wrestle, and in the meantime, tried to build the gym business back up. Jim Crockett was even kind enough to lend me $10,000 to help cover outstanding bills, but by then it was too late. We learned a hard lesson from that experience: if you own a business, you should be there to run it yourself. Once I wasn't around, membership dropped right off, and it never recovered. We ended up having to declare bankruptcy and lost both our house and the gym, which was very unpleasant. It took well into the spring of the following year to get everything settled. Then my wife took our younger son back to Charlotte with her while our oldest, who was now 16, stayed on to finish the last three weeks of school and spend part of the summer with his friends.

In 1979 George Scott decided to revive the Canadian Heavyweight Championship belt. Promoters don't always tell their plans to wrestlers, so at first I didn't know my name was going in the hat for that one. I still looked the part — I was in great shape, and I was already very well known as an "all-Canadian" hero. I was already busy wrestling seven days a week, and then I flew back and forth between Charlotte and Toronto for the lead-up to the Canadian Championship bout. It took about three months to get through all the rounds, and there was an impressive roster of names involved. The first round went: Mad Dog Vachon against Jay Youngblood — Mad Dog pinned Jay for the win. Greg Valentine against Pedro Morales — Greg pinned Pedro after a brainbuster. Jimmy Snuka against Angelo Mosca — Jimmy won by a disqualification after ramming Angelo's head into the ring-post and opening a nasty cut, which made Mosca go berserk and hit referee John Lang. Ricky Steamboat against Brute Bernard — Ricky pinned Brute with a chop to the head. Gene Kiniski won by default over Lord Alfred Hayes when Hayes missed his plane connection and failed to show up.

I wrestled Ken Patera in the first round. Ken and I often got mistaken for each other in Charlotte because we looked so much alike: about the same size, with curly "afro" hair and big legs. I had wrestled Ken before, fairly early in my career. Our first match was in New York when I was on a short tour for Vince McMahon Sr. and the first booking was at Madison Square Garden. I had always liked arriving at matches before everyone got there so I could have a look around, and as I stood in the large, overwhelmingly empty seating area, looking at the incredibly long walk down to the ring, I felt a loneliness unlike anything I'd ever felt in Toronto. I was years past stage fright, but I was nervous about wrestling Ken, who was rapidly making a name for himself as an aggressive heel, and I felt like I needed some extra time to gather my composure and summon some optimism to put on a good match with him. Ken had just won his Olympic bronze medal for weightlifting and he was about 50 pounds heavier than me. He'd become a most impressive wrestler in a relatively short period of time, making his debut in 1973 and developing ring charisma in the AWA under Verne Gagne. Because he'd been a champion weightlifter, he was extremely agile and quick as weightlifters have to be to get that bar overhead with such speed.

After the bell rang for our match and I waited for Ken to talk to the crowd with his body language (which usually takes a wrestler years to learn), much to my surprise we locked up in a perfect referee's hold. I was amazed — Ken's grip was like a feather. Promoters were always concerned about no light showing between two opponents when you were locked up, and it was always a balancing act between exerting enough pressure to keep the hold but not gripping so tight you'd blow yourself up (get winded). That's why amateurs wrestle in three-minute rounds, as opposed to pros, who can go on for an hour if necessary. Ken had a "smooth as silk" style that impressed me immediately, particularly because he hadn't been wrestling for very long, and we went back and forth for about 10 minutes. Then I found myself in Ken's famous swinging full nelson hold and knew it was time to submit and be happy with the performance I had put on. But I also knew I would see him again later.

By the time I wrestled Ken in the Canadian Heavyweight Championship Tournament, his weight had come down from the 290 it had been at the Olympics and he was pretty close to my own weight, 245. I had also been spending a lot of time in Charlotte with a longtime friend of George Scott's: the original Nature Boy, Buddy Rogers, who gave me some very helpful advice on the proper use of the figure-four leg lock, and told me to have confidence in my ability for the tournament. I knew Ken could go to the time limit without taking a second breath so I took my time during our match, trying to keep a slower pace. Ken had shoulder, arm and leg strength on his side but he wasn't much of a flyer, like me. My best move was still the drop kick. I liked to hit my opponents with three in a row then go for a pin, but Ken's upper body strength could throw me four feet in the air if I aimed at his chest. So at about the seven-minute mark, I threw two drop kicks, then went for something he didn't expect and quickly wrapped his legs in the figure-four the way Buddy had told me to. Thank you for the win, Ken — I know payback is hard, but it was a good match and I owe you for that first round.

In the second round, Greg Valentine pinned Mad Dog Vachon with a brainbuster, and Jimmy Snuka and Ricky Steamboat fought an incredible match that ended with Steamboat pinning Snuka after Snuka tried to cradle him. Jimmy had been dominant through the match, but he just couldn't keep Ricky down. At one point Snuka tried a diving headbutt on Steamboat but Steamboat lifted his elbow up and got Snuka square in the face. Steamboat reversed the cradle for the 1-2-3 and the win. When the match was over Snuka was furious at his loss, and gave Steamboat a knee to the throat off the top rope and a piledriver, then put some kind of a nerve hold to Steamboat's throat. This attack went on for several minutes and in the end Steamboat was left in the ring writhing in pain. He was such bad shape that me, Jay Youngblood, Pedro Morales and Angelo Mosca all had to carry him back to the dressing room when it was over. My match was against former NWA champion Gene Kiniski, who had come out of retirement for this tournament. He always bragged about being Canada's number one athlete, playing football for the Edmonton Eskimos and wrestling. I knew I couldn't beat Gene on my best day or his worst day, and that's the way the match went — all his way because he was a veteran pro wrestler. But larger, natural raw-boned strength, endurance and speed had left him vulnerable. After 12 minutes I slipped behind him using a reverse cradle — 1-2-3. I felt great knowing it takes a champion to make a champion.

In the third round Greg Valentine won his match over Ricky

Steamboat by default, because of the injuries inflicted by Snuka. I didn't have to wrestle anyone in this round as it had been decided that the winner of the last two first round pairings only had to win the second round match to advance to the final match. So the title match for the Canadian Heavyweight Championship on September 9, 1979 was me against Greg Valentine, the son of my idol, the great Johnny Valentine. Not my first match with Greg, but the most important, and like my other matches with him, it was hard fought because of his rigid, aggressive style. Like Ken Patera, Greg Valentine knew I had numerous wins with a standing abdominal stretch (as did Greg's dad) but I never went for that hold with either opponent. Instead, I took most of the pounding in both matches and, as Buddy Rogers showed me, I watched for the spot to slip on the figure-four leg lock — and goodbye Greg. After the match Valentine complained to the referee that I was using the ropes for leverage (and if you ask him about it today, he'll still tell you he won that match, not me), but the referee didn't believe him and let the decision stand. The Canadian Heavyweight Championship Title was mine. The proudest moment came when my friend and mentor Whipper Billy Watson said on the microphone that I "would make Canada proud of me," as he presented me with the belt.

For the next year I defended my title at Maple Leaf Gardens against many opponents, including Nick Bockwinkel, Jimmy Snuka, The Destroyer and Greg Valentine. Bockwinkel was the AWA champ at the time, and I also got to wrestle him for the AWA title too, but the match ended in a draw. Jimmy Snuka was the U.S. champion and was unsuccessful at taking the Canadian Title from me — and I won his title from him the second time we grappled for the belt. The following spring I got another shot at the NWA World Heavyweight Title against Harley Race at Maple Leaf Gardens on April 13, 1980. It ended in a draw.

I finally lost the Canadian Heavyweight Championship Title to

The Great Hossein (The Iron Sheik) on May 25th. With the hostage situation in Iran happening then, The Iron Sheik was just too hot a heel to be defeated. Also, Frank Tunney began giving Angelo Mosca a big push as the local hero, and towards the end of 1980, I began to feel like my run as a main-eventer at the Gardens was coming to an end. My last match at Maple Leaf Gardens was against Ray Stevens on June 14, 1981 — and I lost. No DQ. Soon after that I moved to Kansas City and never wrestled at the Gardens again.

I continued to prosper on the Mid-Atlantic circuit, but I was never more than a mid-card wrestler down south. Still, I was making anywhere from $125 to $1,000 a match and won a couple of belts during my time there. On December 12, 1980, I tag-teamed with George Wells to defeat The Sheepherders in Richmond, Virginia, and we claimed the Mid-Atlantic Tag Team Title for ourselves. We held onto the title for a few months before losing to Mr. Fuji and Tenryu on February 7, 1981 in Greensboro. I teamed up with Johnny Weaver next and won it back from them — but then Weaver and I lost it to Nikolai Volkoff and Chris Markoff in June 1981.

My career as a good-time Charlie was humming right along too. I spent a lot of my time hanging out with wrestlers living at the Days Inn outside of Charlotte, and there was a big party scene there. Piper lived there, Jimmy Snuka, Ray Stevens and many others. I only stayed at that Days Inn a few times myself, when I first got to Charlotte and before I left for Kansas City. Since I had my family living with me, we had our own house in Charlotte and I'd go home after I dropped everyone off after the matches. I had a big car, so I helped out driving on the trips, which were often 300-plus miles each way. I continued to drive Cadillacs throughout my time in the South, six of them all told, and they were good for taking four people at a time. A lot of the partying went on in the cars on the way back and forth from the matches.

Yes, there was drinking done in the cars, and drugs were done in the cars, depending on who you were taking, and to this day I don't know how we all got away with it. I can't remember any wrestlers ever being caught and thrown in jail for drinking and driving. The police just seemed to let them go. I never got stopped and I never got in any accidents — someone or something must have been looking out for me then. I'm not promoting or excusing any of this behavior, I'm just telling you what went on. The promoters knew it was going on too, but they subscribed to the belief that any publicity was good publicity, and since pro wrestling has always had kind of an "outlaw" image anyway, if wrestlers were getting into trouble, in their minds it was just more free advertising for the matches.

In Mid-Atlantic all the boys hung around together, even the main eventers, because we all had such hectic schedules. A town this night, and then maybe B and C towns tomorrow, and it mixed us all up. There were different towns every night and two towns on Saturday and Sunday, plus flying back and forth to Toronto. It was a frenetic pace, that's for sure, but it kept us in shape and more importantly, it kept the money coming in. Everybody was being paid at different rates, and while money was a sore point for a lot of the guys, I must say that I wasn't a complainer when it came to payoffs. I never said, "Hey, I deserve $25 or $50 more" to a promoter in my entire life. I knew many wrestlers who did that, and maybe I should have learned how to do it too, because I think that when the promoter found someone like myself who didn't complain, they took advantage of me and took more money than they should have — or didn't give me as much money as I should have received. I was never unemployed, and I didn't like to rock the boat, so I never complained about being underpaid. And so they would keep me on the job but weren't paying me what I was worth. I said before I never made less than $25 a night, but for many years, $65 a match was a lot of money. And as time went on it became $100, and $150, and $250, and so on.

My brother once asked me, "How come you didn't save any money?" It's a legitimate question, but there are a lot of reasons. I moved 38 times in the course of my wrestling career. And if you think of moving across the country every couple of years — 1,400 miles, 2,000 miles, going large distances and having to find a new place to live and buying furniture all the time — it gets expensive. There were times I was paid very well, making $5-6,000 a week, but it wasn't every week. That would be for a short period of time, and then it would be back to low pay again. Wrestling fans or any fans who follow the careers of athletes and entertainers think that everybody makes money. Truth is, it's usually just the main eventers or the top people that make money. The main events were supported by the low-end guys, and they always got a fraction of what the main event guys got. Being a wrestler in the old days required a lot of entrepreneurial skills. What we see today on TV are very large, spectacular, two- to three-hour well-sponsored programs: the wrestlers are all on contracts, and big companies will pay millions to have their stuff advertised on the WWE shows. It was nothing like that in the old days. We had to go out and find our own sponsors, and the territories themselves would be up and down all the time. A territory wouldn't continuously make money for 10 years straight — there was no such thing. If they had a good year, or maybe two, they were doing well. There were certain wrestlers who were always in high demand: The Sheik for instance, who had seven years of top run, and Bobo Brazil, André The Giant, Haystack Calhoun and many others who were always in demand and taken care of very well. But for the territories themselves, even when these people were on the card or headlining the card, it didn't mean much if the territory was in a slump. The promoters would lose a lot of money, but they always went home with something for themselves. Paying the wrestlers came last.

There was no formal pay structure anywhere, and no way to guarantee yourself any kind of steady income in the old days. Nobody would talk to you about putting something aside for your retirement, and of course there was nothing like health benefits or reimbursement for all the traveling to the different towns, which took a lot of money. When you're paying out of your own pocket for gas and maintenance for the car, lodging and food, the expenses add up pretty fast. Promoters never paid for hotels or motels. They never paid for meals either, and to maintain the physique that I had, I had to be an overeater, and eat the right kind of food. I couldn't just survive on hamburgers and road food, I had to supply the house the best I could. And I'm sure there were times when my family went without — I know that for sure, because my wife always considered that I came first, whether it would be buying clothes or food. In the days of my early wrestling, you couldn't go around to a lot of stores and just find stuff on sale, like you can today. So clothes were sometimes very costly, and because of my physique, I had to get a lot of custom-made clothes for a dress-up territory where I wore suits. Whipper Watson wore suits all the time, so I had to wear them too when I was out with him. It wasn't until I got down south that guys used to just run around in blue jeans and didn't care about what they wore. But if you cared about your appearance, clothes cost a lot of money, cars cost a lot of money, long trips required gas and sometimes you never made more than enough for what it cost for the gas and a little bit to take home.

Plus you were completely at the mercy of the promoter when it came to bookings and getting paid, and the promoters always made sure they got their cut first. When they got a chance to take advantage of someone like me (and I was not the only one by a long shot), who didn't complain because they were just thankful for the job, they took it. Promoters never really fire anybody either — I know I never lost a job in 32 years, even though I didn't play politics very well. If a promoter didn't want to use you anymore, he'd just cut back the bookings and/or keep bumping you down the card until you weren't making enough money and you'd leave the territory on your own. I was certainly valuable enough to every promotion I worked for to keep a job and keep myself in a decent position on the card. Whenever I started feeling like my run in a promotion was up, I always did what my good friend Jimmy Snuka used to say: "Get on the phone and call somebody." I never left a promotion with hard feelings, but I watched a lot of other wrestlers go out of the business that way, until they finally found out that there was nowhere else they could go because nobody wanted to use them, or that they didn't have enough talent, or got tired of taking the abuse.

The uncertainty of the financial situation week to week was not helped by the fact that, growing up, I had never learned to save money — so it never entered my mind to do it when I was on the road. I believe that one has to be taught to save money, and that is definitely something parents have to do. Anyway, I never learned, so whenever I had a lot of money coming in, it seemed to burn a hole in my pocket. I came from a family that didn't have a lot of money, and I had been working full-time since I was 15 years old. My mother did say one thing to me: "Save money for a rainy day," but that's about all she taught me. She lived pay to pay while I was growing up and I did the same thing for my whole wrestling career — living from pay to pay, hoping and not knowing at this point whether I satisfied my children in what they needed in life. I made sure they were involved in lots of sports, lacrosse, baseball and hockey and soccer, and those things cost money, so I hope they're satisfied with what their father provided. I don't know what my wife would say. She never, ever complained, and she always looked great wherever we were going. I have to say that I am a victim of being very extravagant when it comes to money too, it's part of the manic aspect of being a manic-depressive. I've given cars away to people about half-a-dozen times. Another part of it was also spending a lot of time around guys that were making a lot of money and I wanted to pay my way, so if it's your turn to buy a round of drinks, or pay for a meal, well . . . I remember Gene Kiniski telling me that when you're the champion that's when it costs you the most money, because you're expected to pay for everything. I was the champion quite a few times, and I believed that image was very important to me as a professional wrestler.

CHAPTER SEVEN

Kansas City All-Star

Towards the end of the summer of 1981, I got a call from former NWA Champion Pat O'Connor. Pat was a consummate scientific wrestler, and he was now the booker for Bob Geigel's Central States territory, based out of Kansas City, Missouri. Pat had seen me wrestle in St. Louis, and invited me to come and wrestle for the Central States promotion, which ran shows in Kansas and Missouri, and extended out into Nebraska, Iowa and Illinois. If I went there, I would also be on the cards for Sam Muchnick's promotion in St. Louis, which was still a first-rate city. I had been on Sam's television show *Wrestling at the Chase* many times during my early days, and Central States had their own show, *All-Star*

Wrestling. More World Championship matches were booked, won or lost in this territory than any other place: the list of champions includes Ed "Strangler" Lewis; Lou Thesz; Bill Longson; Whipper Billy Watson; Buddy Rogers; Gene Kiniski; Dory Funk Jr.; Jack Brisco; Terry Funk; Dusty Rhodes and Ric Flair.

Both Sam and Bob had been NWA Presidents during the time when it was one of the most powerful positions in the wrestling business. They ran their territories to complement each other instead of trying to compete head-to-head, and this approach actually provided more professional opportunities and exposure for wrestlers in both territories. Sam's shows were more old-school than Bob's — he didn't really like gimmicks or angles — and since I was such a good scientific wrestler, I got a big push on Sam's cards. Bob, on the other hand, preferred angles and character wrestlers, and he had a lot more titles up for grabs: the Television Title, the Central States Champion and Tag Team Champion Titles, where Sam just had the Missouri State Title, which was won or lost only in St. Louis.

Sam Muchnick was one of wrestling's living legends. He came into the wrestling business like a lot of promoters — from newspaper sports departments. Sam started out as a high-profile sports writer at a time when wrestling promoters relied heavily on newspapermen for publicity. This was before television, when everybody read the newspaper for the results, so the sports reporter was very important to get the match write-ups in. Writers became very valuable to the office as promotional people, and a lot of them took the next logical step and became promoters themselves. After every match, Sam Muchnick would have his phone going so people could call in for the results, and there would be stories in the paper the next day.

Sam had also been one of the founding members of the NWA, and for decades St. Louis was the center of the wrestling world. Sam brought in talent from around the country to work his shows at the world-famous Kiel Auditorium on Friday nights, and he controlled the bookings of the NWA World champion for many years. Sometimes he'd run a little town in Illinois once in while. That would make an extra few dollars for the guest wrestlers because he flew them all in, the top ones in from every territory. And later on he added the TV show and the people would fill up Kiel Auditorium, and when he went out to the arena they'd fill that up. He was probably the best payoff man in the wrestling world. I can't say this for certain, but I've heard way back before my time when wrestling first started the promoters paid out tremendous amounts of money. Then they learned — *well hey, we'd better keep some for ourselves* — so the payoff structure changed, with the promoters taking a lot more off the top.

★ ★ ★

I have to say I was warned from the start not to go to Kansas City. A lot of people said to me, "You don't want to go there," and after I'd been there a few weeks I found out why. But there was that irresistible lure of another shot at the NWA World Heavyweight Championship Title. Pat had held the title himself in 1959, and Harley Race, who also worked out of Central States, had held the title six times at that point and recently had it taken from him by Dusty Rhodes. I had wrestled Harley many times, and I'd already challenged him for the World Title in Toronto the previous year. I really thought my time had come and that Kansas City was the place I'd finally achieve my career pinnacle. So I made my decision. I sent my wife and sons on ahead to find us a place to live and get settled in, and I left Charlotte a week later.

To this day, I don't know if I did the right thing by leaving the Carolinas for Central States. I was doing well in Mid-Atlantic, I could have had a long run there, but I was torn between going with Dusty Rhodes and his crew, or staying and opposing Ric Flair, who didn't want anything to do with me. Don't get me wrong, I got along well with Ric most of the time. When he came to the Carolinas from the AWA in the mid-1970s he had the whole package going for him: he was flamboyant, great on the microphone, put a lot of effort into his wrestling and if anyone was destined to be a World Champion, it was Ric Flair. Just before I got to Kansas City in September of 1981, Ric won the NWA World Heavyweight Title from Dusty Rhodes, and held onto it for nearly two years. I wrestled Ric only one time when he wasn't the champion, and I have a photo where he's walking away from the ring a winner — but not joyously. You can see in the picture that he wasn't happy with the way the match went at all, and I think that's when I killed any chance I had at the World Title. I knew going into that match that I would make sure I made Ric look good but I also made myself look good too, and I don't think he liked that very much. And so looking back now, that's probably when the word went down the line to the NWA promoters that I couldn't be controlled, and I sabotaged my final chance to be World Champion. Still, it took two years for that truth to sink in.

So off I went to Kansas City. It turned out to be a mixed blessing. I got a good push immediately as a contender for the World Championship, won a Central States tag title with Rufus R. Jones right away and won it back again later with Steve Regal as my partner. I won the Television Title from Mean Gene Lewis right away too and held it for quite a while, losing it back to him about four months later. My old foe from Tri-State, Jerry Brown, was in Kansas City while I was there and I wrestled him a lot. Mike George and I tagged against Jerry Brown and David Von Erich in May 1982 — with me not knowing how important the Von Erichs would become in my future. But it was obvious even then that David was going to be a huge star. All the Von Erich boys were under the influence of their father Fritz (Jack

Adkisson), but David was the only one who had the strength to get out from under his father's thumb for awhile and go on the road by himself, spending some very productive time with Dory Funk Jr. in the Florida territory. David had been wrestling along with his brother Kevin for four or five years already, but the time away from home playing a heel put a polish on his wrestling and gave him an edge that was very noticeable when he returned. David was making his way back to Texas by the time I wrestled him, and following his return, Dallas would explode as a major wrestling center.

I had another memorable tag match later that same year in St. Louis — Greg Valentine and myself against Hulk Hogan and Dick The Bruiser. I mention this match because when people find out I wrestled in the WWF they *always* ask if I wrestled Hulk Hogan. Always. So there's your answer. Yes, but not in the WWF — and we lost the match.

One thing I got to do in Kansas City that I'd never done before was a major heel turn. I had dabbled with it in Mid-Atlantic, and it felt like the right time for it in KC. I had wrestled as an aggressive babyface so long, and got so good at it that I was now wrestling a lot of heels that were new. You see, normally it's the heel who runs the match, and runs it his way. But since I was the experienced veteran, when I got in the ring with a new heel I would have to lead him in a match even though it wasn't my job — and it also meant the outcome would probably be favorable to me. There were always new heels breaking in and I would beat a lot of these guys, but I'd have to lead them. So turning heel was a logical progression for me. I was now older than most of the new guys, which means something because usually the older guy is in charge of the match and if he's a heel, he's really in charge. So this liberated me in a sense, gave me a chance to do interviews — something I still wasn't really competent at, because I had managers to do it for me before this and I still didn't know how to interview as well as I would later on. But I did know how to control a match, because now I could play to the crowd and turn the crowd any way I wanted to. Playing heel released my inhibitions, allowing me to do things I wanted to do and knew how to do but couldn't as a babyface. I could be the Dewey that was inside of me, after many years of wrestling other heels.

One of the new young guys who came on the scene when I was in Kansas City was Ray "Hercules" Hernandez. He came in about the same time as Mark Romero, son of Ricky Romero, and I wrestled them both a lot. Hercules was in his learning years, and very willing to do what he was told. During my matches with Hercules, I would talk to him in the ring in a low whisper as wrestlers do, telling him what I was going to do, how he should react, calling high spots and he would follow my lead. For some reason this used to really upset Bob Geigel, who would be sitting close to the ring so he could see how hard his talent was working. Bob told me very bluntly "I don't want you talking to Herc in the ring anymore, I want him to do it on his own." After that I continued to call my matches with Hercules as usual, but I made sure Bob couldn't see me talking to him. I can't say if that was just me being obstinate or knowing instinctively that Hercules still needed help whether Bob Geigel liked it or not (just like Bob told me what to do in the matches in St. Louis when I used to wrestle him — something you forgot about, Bob!), but it still made for good matches. I enjoyed Herc as a partner because we fit well together, and he worked very hard. When I turned heel, Herc and I won the Central States Tag Title (the third time for me) from Mike George and Mark Romero. Mark Romero was also someone very easy to control in the ring and have good matches with. Mark was basically quite content to be in the ring where his dad wanted him to be, while his brother wrestled in Charlotte as Jay Youngblood.

Herc and I wrestled one match as heels inside a fort near

Kansas City. I wrestled in a number of forts during my career — Fort Sumter, Fort Sill, Fort Smith — which I always found interesting, because not everybody gets to see the inside of one. This particular match was held inside a very large barracks with bleachers packed on all four sides, seating about 2,000 Marines in all, divided into groups of active Marines and Marines with their wives and families. Instead of clapping or booing, the Marines, who all had very closely shaved heads, would call out Marine chants in response to the matches. This one turned out to be a very scary match for Herc and myself because we won by cheating, and the tone of the Marines changed to very loud disapproval at our victory. As we left the ring, led through a very narrow aisle between the bleachers by a group of MPs, the noise and aggression was the most threatening I have ever experienced after any match, short of a riot. At that moment I found myself in the aisle where the bleachers met and turning around to face these agitated Marines head-on, I threatened and aggravated them more. Later I realized what a dumb move that was, because as we were ushered away, I noticed the disciplined Marine soldiers never left the bleachers.

Because of Bob's attitude about me leading Hercules through matches, the biggest surprise I had in Kansas City was being allowed to lead the matches when I wrestled Harley Race, who was the hometown babyface and an extremely talented champion. I believe he let me do it because of my hard work and my development as a very aggressive heel. I was very proud of wrestling Harley and having my hand raised twice.

The big problem in Kansas City wasn't the work or the titles, it was lack of money. There was plenty of work, but the payoffs were much lower than I had been getting in Mid-Atlantic. After only two weeks, my wife was telling me we were going to starve to death if we stayed there, and she turned out to be right. I don't want to put Bob Geigel down by saying he didn't know what he was doing — he was good in the ring — but as a promoter, I suppose he worried about his pocketbook more. Some promoters start with nothing and get to the top, but Bob spent so much time worrying about money he didn't have anything left to put into promoting. I remember him saying the only thing he regretted about being a wrestling promoter is that he had to put so much money of his own into running the territory. Also, the Central States territory was owned jointly by Bob, Harley Race and Pat O'Connor, which meant three hands in the pie and therefore not much left for the wrestlers.

Sam Muchnick's payoffs were still high in 1981. I got $500 or more in St. Louis just for being on the bottom of the card, but then Sam retired on New Year's Day 1982, with a big farewell show at the Checkerdome. I wrestled Baron Von Raschke on that card. St. Louis was bought out by a consortium of partners including Verne Gagne, Bob Geigel, Harley Race, Pat O'Connor, and Gene Kiniski. Pat O'Connor retired from wrestling that same day to take over the St. Louis office, and inside of a year the payoffs were down to $95 for the middle of the card. To put it in perspective, the first year I wrestled for Central States I made $19,000. By the second year it was down to $16,000 — and I was in the office every day asking for an advance of $50 just to survive. My wife had a job too, and she still ended up hocking her jewelry — not to party or buy new clothes, but to pay for groceries. That's how bad our situation became.

So I was working all the time, wrestling three or four times a week, but I was not making any money. The shortage, however, didn't stop me from continuing to drink heavily and smoke marijuana. Kansas City was where the addiction really began to get its hooks into me. In the Carolinas I drank and smoked marijuana because I was feeling good and wanted to feel better. In Kansas City, I was trying to drown my increasing feeling of desperation at being constantly broke and having the World Title dangled in front of me, then given to someone else. That was another lesson. There's two types of self abuse: when you're feeling good and want to feel better; and then when you're feeling bad and you want to escape from it for a while. I never thought taking one joint, one drink, one of anything at a party would lead to two, or three or four. And from my experiences talking to other addicts in rehab and recovery, nobody really knows when the addiction begins to take over. By the time you realize you're hooked, it's already too late to stop. And continued steroid use just poured more fuel on the fire of all my resentments over the lack of money and being passed over for the World Title again and again.

Following the pattern I started in Charlotte, I continued to take my anger and frustration out on my wife. I wasn't home very much but when I was, I was always in a fighting mood. I started to abuse her verbally and physically. I blamed her for all the problems I was having with work, when they were entirely my fault. The substance abuse was also beginning to interfere with my work ethic. I'd sleep in or get lost on my way to matches and be late, then stay out for hours after they ended. One night I wrestled at a place only about 5-10 minutes from our condo and didn't get home until nine the next morning — and when my wife asked where I'd been and how I got home, I honestly couldn't remember. Another time I just left my car on the Interstate facing the wrong way. Someone must have been looking out for me because I got home safely that time too but I couldn't tell you how. This sort of irresponsible behavior was completely out of character for me, but it shows how the addiction was taking over my personality.

* * *

I hung on in Kansas City, waiting for my promised NWA World Heavyweight Title shots. I had been slowly building up to it with my Television and Central States Tag Title wins, and building up my reputation as a heel. I did a really nasty heel turn at a match in St. Louis in the fall of 1982 — Dusty Rhodes, Bruce Reed and myself were tagging against Kim Duk, Ken Patera and Ray Hernandez. Dusty and I were in the ring together and he missed an elbow smash and hit me by mistake, opening up my head. I turned on him in anger and began pummeling him.

Ric Flair was in and out of Kansas City several times during the first six months of 1983 to defend the World Heavyweight Title, but never against me. I won the Central States Heavyweight Champion Title from Manny Fernandez early in the year and held onto it for nearly six months — I lost it very briefly to Bulldog Bob Brown in May but won it back in about a week, then lost it for good to Harley Race in June. In May 1983, I thought I was still considered in the running for a World Title match against Ric Flair, but when Ric came back to defend the title again in June, it was against Harley Race — and Harley won. I was given a title match with Harley not long after he won it from Ric, and I lost. Well, it was Harley's territory and that's the way it went.

At that point I knew then I had to get out of Kansas City for good. As hard as I was trying to escape reality by drinking, drugging and partying, it was becoming painfully clear that I was never going to win the NWA World Heavyweight Title and our financial situation was getting too desperate to ignore. We hadn't paid the rent on our condo for two months because we were so short of money, and ended up having to sneak out in the middle of the night with our furniture, which we stored in a friends' garage while we stayed with them a few nights and decided what to do. I had been talking to my friend and frequent opponent Mean Gene Lewis, who had left Kansas City the year before and was having a very successful run as The Mongol in World Class Championship Wrestling (WCCW) in Dallas. I had suggested to Gene that he might make a good Mongol because he was built a lot like Geeto Mongol (Newt Tattrie) whom I'd known in

Toronto, and Gene had actually toured Nigeria with Geeto as one of the Mongols for a bit before he went to Texas. He was wrestling as a solo Mongol in Texas, so I thought I could go down there and be his partner, make it a tag team again. Gene told me straight out there was no room in World Class for another heel, but I was determined to get out of Kansas City and find better paying work. I thought Texas was the place to do it.

The way I see it, there wasn't really any other decision I could have made. I was not going to get anywhere if I stayed in Central States. That fact had finally sunk into my addiction-fogged brain. World Class was *the* hot territory in 1983, so I figured I had nothing to lose by trying my luck there. I didn't even tell Bob Geigel in person that I was leaving. I just left a note under the office door that said: "Can't pay the rent. Leaving Kansas City. See you soon."

The family was down to me, my wife and our younger son — our older son had married and moved into his own apartment with his new wife. My wife certainly didn't need any convincing to leave Kansas City. Even though we were broke and there was no guarantee of any work for me in Texas, she hated Kansas City, and more to the point, the person I had become while we were there. She said much later I wasn't the man she had married anymore. I had become mean and selfish and thought I knew it all. And she was absolutely right, but there was no telling me that at the time. And it was going to get much worse.

So once again we packed up everything and put our furniture in storage until we knew where we were going to be living. We left Kansas City almost two years to the day we arrived, with little more than the clothes on our backs and what we could fit in the car, and headed south to Texas.

CHAPTER EIGHT

The Birth of The Missing Link

When we got to Gene and Pam Lewis' place in Bowie, Texas, Gene was away until the next night. I insisted that Pam shave my head right away, even though she was nervous and wanted to wait until Gene got back. It was the weekend and I wanted to go into Dallas and see Fritz Von Erich, owner of WCCW, first thing on Monday about getting some work. I made Pam shave everything off except for two little "Mongol" tufts on the forehead and back of the head. I have naturally curly sandy-red hair and had worn it many styles and lengths — close-cropped early in my career, longer in the 1970s when that became the style — but never anything this extreme. My younger son thought it looked really cool, but Pam and my wife both burst out laughing and Pam said "Your head looks like a light bulb." When Gene got back Saturday night after his show and found me sitting in his chair, grinning with my bald head and Mongol tufts, he said the same thing he'd said when I phoned him a couple of weeks earlier to tell him I was coming down to be his partner: "You're crazy! There's no room here," meaning that the promotion already had all the heels and babyfaces matched up and they didn't need anyone extra. But I was determined that I was going to succeed in the Dallas territory.

On Monday my wife and son drove with me into Dallas and waited in the stifling hot car for two hours while I met with Fritz. Fritz laughed out loud when he saw my haircut too and asked, "What are you supposed to be?" I can't blame him, it didn't really go with the light summer suit I had on, and I hadn't taken any time to work on the gimmick beyond the hair. Fritz confirmed what Gene had told me, that there wasn't any room for another wrestler right them but while I was in his office, Ernie "The Big Cat" Ladd called from Mid-South Wrestling, which had taken over most of Leroy McGuirk's old Tri-State territory in Louisiana, Mississippi and Oklahoma — the same area where I had wrestled in the early '70s, tag-teaming with Dennis Stamp. Ernie was calling because one of their wrestlers had walked out and they needed an experienced substitute heel to wrestle against Magnum T.A. that night in New Orleans. That was all I needed to hear. I ran back out to the car and my wife drove me straight to the airport.

Now I have to ask you this: would I have gotten that job if I had listened to Gene and not bothered to go see Fritz that day? I took it as a sign that I had made the right decision. I had no reservations about dropping everything to go work with Ernie Ladd, whom I'd known for a long time. Ernie was one of wrestling's biggest stars of the 1960s and 1970s, in both status and size — he stood 6'10" tall and weighed over 300 pounds. Now he was booking and managing wrestlers for Mid-South, which was owned by Cowboy Bill Watts. Bill had been Tri-State's undisputed star wrestler when I was there with Dennis Stamp in the early '70s. Not long after I left in 1973, Bill walked out on McGuirk and went to Florida, taking the North American Title belt with him for a couple of years, to wrestle for Eddie Graham. Bill returned to Tri-State in 1975 and slowly took over booking and running of the territory until he got McGuirk to sell out to him in 1979.

Pretty well everyone agrees that Bill Watts was a brilliant promoter, possibly one of the best ever. Anything you've seen in wrestling in the last 20 years, Bill Watts thought of first. Bill had pulled out of the NWA not long after taking over from McGuirk, but aside from losing the World Title matches it didn't appear to hurt the promotion much. Bill had a way with new talent too, and by 1983 he had created a stable of some of wrestling's most memorably outrageous characters: Ted DiBiase; Paul Orndorff; The Fabulous Freebirds; The Junkyard Dog; Jake "The Snake" Roberts; Kamala The Ugandan Giant; King Kong Bundy; Butch Reed and Jim Duggan, not to mention the Cowboy himself.

I also had a huge amount of respect for Bill Watts as a businessman — he ran a good, tight ship financially, which was a relief after my experience in Kansas City, and looked after his wrestlers well. But I also have to say I found him an extremely tough taskmaster. I remember Leroy McGuirk as one of the fairest men in the wrestling business. Bill was fair too, but he did not like people costing him money unnecessarily, so he would do things like fine a wrestler $500 for missing a match even if the payoff was only $150. I learned this the hard way, but I also never missed another match again. When The Link was billed as having the "hardest head in wrestling," I became known for using it to break a lot of things. However, I stopped breaking folding tables with my head when Bill Watts started charging me $60 per table. Another time Bill had these satin promotional jackets made up that had "Mid-South Wrestling" on the back and started asking people "Who wants a jacket?" I liked them, so I said "I do" and he handed me one. I thought that was the end of it, but the on the next paycheck I got, there was an $80 deduction — for the jacket. (By the way Bill, I still have that jacket — the zipper's broken and there's a hole in one of the pockets!)

One thing Bill did that I don't remember any other promoter doing was taking money in escrow for the top performers. Bill didn't pay me exactly what I should have been paid when I was one of the top guys — he had certain friends he paid more and I still hadn't learned how to ask for more money — but with the escrow, at least when you left the territory you'd have a chunk of money coming to you, which was a big help.

I made it from Dallas to New Orleans in time for the match that night, and it went fine. Magnum T.A. (Terry Allen) was a young mid-card wrestler who had just come in from the Florida territory and they were grooming him to be a big star. I guess he was also a protégé of Dusty Rhodes, which may have had some influence on the push he was getting from Bill Watts. But after the match in New Orleans, Ernie Ladd said to me "That's the last time you'll be doing a job." Ernie saw when I wrestled Magnum T.A. that night that I was the far superior talent because I had the years of experience behind me and I led Terry through the match. Since there was nothing back in Dallas for me as yet, I decided to stay in Louisiana for a while.

I called my wife the next day at Pam and Gene's place and told her I'd be at Mid-South for a few months, so she and my son drove to Shreveport and checked into the Red Roof Inn off Interstate 35 where all the wrestlers in the territory stayed. She had to borrow $100 from Gene and Pam to make the trip, that's how broke we still were. They stayed there a few days while I wrestled, then Grizzly Smith, Jake "The Snake" Roberts' dad, invited us to stay at his house in Shreveport until we found a place to live and we gratefully accepted his offer. We lived with him for about a month until my wife and son found an apartment in Bossier City, a suburb of Shreveport. While they were apartment-hunting I was working, drinking and smoking marijuana so they hardly saw me.

Soon we got settled in Bossier City and life got back to what was normal for us. Jason started school, and I got down to work. There were still a lot of familiar faces in Mid-South from my time there in the early '70s. Besides Bill Watts and Ernie Ladd there was my old pal General Skandor Akbar, who was managing a fearsome team of heels called Devastation Inc., which included Kamala The Ugandan Giant and King Kong Bundy and which I joined as the proto-Missing Link. Skandor himself had been a top heel going on 15 years. He was actually an American of Lebanese descent, and during the 1970s energy crisis he provoked the wrath of Southern wrestling fans by adopting the persona of a rich Arab oil sheik. The act was so convincing people would throw rocks and sticks at him after matches, slash his tires and chase him in their cars. However, outside the ring he was an exceptionally nice man. The Skandor I knew would do things like read the paper out loud while we were driving the long distances to and from matches, and insert the names of the people in the car into the stories to make us laugh. "In the White House today, the Senators Dewey Robertson and John Mantell voted on a bill . . ." He would keep everyone laughing and awake the whole trip. I was very happy to be working with him again. And my old "enemy" Buddy Roberts, the former Hollywood Blonde who had become a Fabulous Freebird, was in Mid-South too. I scared Buddy the first time he saw me in the dressing room as The Link. He was looking at me very intently, and knowing there was no way he would recognize me as Dewey Robertson, I grabbed my hair and did a Link pose to intimidate him. He didn't back down though, and finally he got enough nerve together to walk across the room and look me right in the face. I couldn't keep up the pose any longer. I started laughing and hugged him and said, "Buddy, it's Dewey Robertson." He was flabbergasted — he really had no idea it was me.

Most people associate The Missing Link with World Class Championship Wrestling, but it was in Mid-South where the gimmick really took shape. I wish I could tell you who came up with the name, but nobody can remember now. It could have been Ernie, Bill Watts or Ken Mantell, the booker, because I got a lot of help from all of them developing the gimmick. Bill was also taking care of the Road Warriors in Atlanta, and told us all at that same time we need to put some kind of paint on our faces. I respected Bill's opinion so I gave it a try. It took a couple of months of different things — sometimes I was "Mad Max The Missing Link" (the Mel Gibson movie of the same name was popular around that time) with a brown and black face — but after a while I settled on the green face with the blue around the eyes. Using the skills I had learned cutting fur coats in my pre-wrestling days, I created matching black fur boots, elbows and kneepads. I also grew a goatee to make myself look more freakish. I know goatees are very common nowadays, but they sure weren't in the 1980s, and I dyed my beard and tufts of hair black. I stole the goatee style from another wrestler, Ox Baker, who was a true main-eventer with many years in the business, and also a very good friend of mine. He was nearing the end of his career when I became The Link, but I did get to see him in a few dressing rooms before he finished. The first time he looked up and saw his beard on me, he just about fell off the bench laughing.

To give credit where credit is due though, I have to say Ken Mantell was the one responsible for The Link's distinctive wrestling style — or more accurately, lack of style. Ken Mantell was a veteran Olympic-style wrestler and former NWA World Junior Heavyweight Champ who had recently retired from the ring to become a booker, and would go on to become one of the most influential and innovative bookers of the 1980s. Ken always had a good sense of what the fans wanted and what looked good on TV, and he told me to forget about all the technical stuff I was so good at, and use my large size and strength to charge at people and throw them off guard. The funny thing is, being such a good ring technician gave me an advantage over the other wrestlers, because I could size up their abilities quickly and anticipate their wrestling moves before they had a chance to apply them. This allowed me to catch them off guard and surprise them by using my head as a weapon to parts of their bodies I felt were most vulnerable.

The Link's notorious head butts came from my friendship with the late Bobo Brazil, who had a very famous finishing move he called the "coco-butt," a flurry of butts to the opponent's head. Doing the head butts in a flurry was a very effective maneuver, so I made it The Link's trademark move too. I also learned quickly that if I banged chairs or broke anything wooden with my head without selling any kind of reaction, people would believe it really didn't hurt me. It worked so well a ¾-inch lump grew on my head that would continually split open, and my hair still hasn't completely grown back on that spot. My study of Johnny Valentine's methods paid off here too. I'd noticed that Johnny could make very few moves but still tie someone up in knots, so I pared my style down to just a few simple moves. What usually happened was I would deliver several battering-ram head butts in a row to my opponent's body to divert his attention — most of the time only one or maybe two to the head to jar the equilibrium — which would allow me to pick him up for a surprise body slam of a very unusual style that had a stunning effect and a quick 1-2-3 count.

I also borrowed some moves from Geeto Mongol. I remembered he used to grab his ponytail and wave it at the crowd, so I would get the crowd going by jumping up on the ropes in a corner of the ring, staring blankly out into the audience, then grabbing the tuft of hair on the back of my head and roaring. I'd also do it before I charged at somebody. By the way, Geeto claims

I used to say this about his gimmick with the ponytail back in Pittsburgh: "I don't know how you guys do that. *I'd* never do a thing like that!" So there you go. Later on I added things like stomping up and down in the ring, almost like I was throwing a tantrum, bringing my knees way up high and landing hard on the ring floor to rev up the crowd.

The result was it didn't take long to stack up win after win against many opponents, who were pinned for the count before they could figure out what was happening to them. Due to my new outlandish appearance, wild antics and unorthodox wrestling style, The Link was an overnight success (though one with 15 years of experience behind it!) and I became a main event contender and star almost immediately. I never had this kind of notoriety as plain old good-guy Dewey Robertson. Somehow, this primitive beast-man had broken through where Dewey couldn't. Being with Mid-South meant I got booked for shows by Paul Boesch in Houston too, which completed my tour of the four meccas of wrestling. Remember? I started in Toronto, had just spent two years in and around St. Louis, had wrestled in New York off and on since the late 1960s for Vince McMahon Sr. — and The Link finally got me to Houston.

Bill Watts helped stir up interest in The Link by hinting to fans that I was someone they should know. When he called the matches, he would say that he was sure he knew The Link from the past, but couldn't put his finger on who it was. Nobody ever connected The Link to Dewey Robertson though, because it was such a radical transformation. I still had the same physique but the hairstyle and makeup hid me completely, even from other wrestlers who had known me for decades. At first I still talked in the ring too, yelling at refs and so on, but as the idea of The Link as a primitive caveman developed, I gradually stopped talking to anybody. I had Skandor talk for me when I was in the ring and talking had never been one of my strengths anyway. I couldn't run off at the mouth the way guys like Roddy Piper or Michael Hayes could. As I ceased speaking or making eye contact with fans or other wrestlers, I also began walking like I imagined a Neanderthal man would walk — slowly and deliberately, but with an aggressive demeanor.

I came to see The Link as one of the true gimmicks, like The Mighty Igor or Haystack Calhoun, that stayed gimmicks at all times. That meant I couldn't just dress up as The Link to go in the ring and then go back on the streets as myself again, it would ruin the effect. I had to be The Link 24/7, very intimidating, not speaking or looking at anybody. One Sunday Butch Reed and I were leaving an afternoon match in Monroe, Louisiana, to go to another one about 100 miles away. I was driving, still wearing the full Link costume: fur elbow and knee pads, fur boots, black shorts, and painted face, so I could go right into the ring when we got there. Just outside Monroe we got pulled over by a cop who parked about five spaces back and walked up to our driver's side. He was short, but intimidating — mirrored glasses, black uniform with gold hardware — and then I got out of the car dressed as The Link. I didn't say anything to him. The cop looked me up and down, then said, "Go ahead" and waved us on. To this day I don't know if he recognized me or just didn't want to confront the situation, but I'd like to think he was a wrestling fan.

Not having to speak or make eye contact had a side benefit for my addictions as well: it relieved me of the responsibility of having to interact with other people, which made it easier for me to retreat further into the shelter of alcohol and marijuana. No one could know if I was drunk or high if I never said anything. I started getting my wife to drive me to shows so I wouldn't have to worry about being sober enough to drive myself home, even though the narrow roads in Louisiana and frequent heavy rains made her very nervous. I was less and less interested in her thoughts and feelings as The Link's popularity exploded. Now it was all about me: my career, my drinking, my drugs. And she just kept on taking it, waiting up until long after midnight to make me dinner after a show, driving me around, tolerating my increasingly abusive and promiscuous behavior and dealing with the outside world for me so I wouldn't have to break the persona of The Link.

★ ★ ★

Sometime in October of 1983, Fritz Von Erich called to say WCCW wanted me back in a month. My wife and I had just celebrated our 20th wedding anniversary. At the same time, Dusty Rhodes was trying to talk me into going to Florida with him to wrestle as "Mad Max" — but I wasn't that comfortable with the kind of wrestling he was into, and I wasn't sure I wanted to take that risk while I was still developing a new image. There was a lot of traffic between Mid-South and WCCW anyway, so going there wasn't really like leaving at all — I would still be part of Devastation Inc.

WCCW was still red-hot when I got there, riding the crest of popularity that had begun the previous Christmas, with the explosive feud between the Von Erich brothers and The Fabulous Freebirds still going strong. The Freebirds — Michael Hayes, the late Terry Gordy, and Buddy Roberts — were an incredible heel team, and I don't think wrestling had seen anything like them before or since. The Freebirds first appeared in the Mid-South territory in 1979 and had a successful run in Georgia too before landing in World Class in late 1982. Each one had his own individual strengths and together they had a great internal chemistry. Michael Hayes was never much of a wrestler, but he had the rock-star looks and swaggering attitude that the women liked and the men resented, and he was great on the microphone. Terry Gordy was the muscle — he was incredibly strong and surprisingly fast for such a big guy. He was an amazing natural talent, and it's a real tragedy that we lost him so young. Buddy Roberts was the experienced ring veteran who anchored the team. He took a lot of bumps, did a lot of jobbing to make the others look good and he was always the "sneaky" Freebird. Buddy was a good-looking guy too, but in a more classic way than Michael Hayes. Their rock 'n' roll party-animal image played well against the clean-cut Von Erich brothers, and because there were three of them, they were good at keeping the advantage on the Von Erichs — but not always beating them, because the Von Erichs were hard to beat.

Devastation Inc. played the role of counter-heels against The Freebirds. When we wrestled the Von Erichs we were heels, but if we wrestled The Freebirds, most people would root for them against us, mainly because of Skandor. When I first got there I often teamed with Kamala The Ugandan Giant, and Skandor was portrayed as the real villain with us just stooges completely under his control. Being part of Devastation Inc. always made me think of what wrestlers used to say in the old days when giants, midgets, geeks, freaks and bears made up our card: "The circus is coming to town." That would be going through my head whenever the entire Devastation entourage — Skandor, me, Kamala, my valet Sheena and Kamala's handler Friday — entered the ring.

Gorgeous Jimmy Garvin was another great heel I tagged with a fair bit. All those Texas tough guys hated his flashy outfits and snooty attitude, and it got worse as the feud between him and David Von Erich heated up over the Texas title. Jimmy wore crazy sequined robes and feather boas over white tights and boots, and he would have his valet Precious disinfect the ring area with a sequined spray can, then remove his robes and fix his hair before he would get in the ring.

The World Class faces were a pretty formidable lot too: Iceman King Parsons, Chris Adams, Bruiser Brody, Brian Adias, John Mantell, and of course the mighty Von Erich brothers. I remember all the Von Erich boys as real tough customers, whether I was wrestling them one-on-one or in a tag match. Their father Fritz was a giant of a man with a heart like a lion. In his wrestling days he played the character of a German after the Second World War and was one of the most hated (and popular) heels for the first 15 years of his career. He was relentless against his opponents and he passed that attitude onto his sons when they got to be wrestling age. Fritz made sure the boys knew how important it was for them never to be crushed or beaten down in the ring and they understood exactly what their dad said. They knew they were the promoter's sons and their opponents would make them look good, but they still couldn't take a chance and so they had this powerful aggression built into them. Each brother was just a couple years older or younger than the one before — Kevin, the oldest and the first to start wrestling, was the most aggressive and when the others came after him, they knew the pattern they had to follow. When people say to me now "I saw you wrestle Kerry Von Erich in one of the promo videos and you pummeled him," I don't believe I really pummeled him, because we weighed about the same and he was at least 20 years younger than me. I just *kept on him*, as we say in the business, not letting up, just giving a little bit to him to keep the excitement level high. The one thing the Von Erichs were really known for was not *selling* (making a blow look like it hurt) for their opponents, because they knew better than to show any weakness — so you really did have to keep on them to make a match look good. Kerry, Kevin and David, whether solo or together in tag team matches, were more than a handful.

Besides a great pool of talent, a major part of WCCW's success was its extended TV presence. It was the first regional promotion to have both local and nationally syndicated TV shows, even before the WWF, so people all across the country could watch its matches. The show was broadcast by Channel 39, the Dallas affiliate of the Christian Broadcasting Network, and its producers pioneered the use of multiple cameras, instant replays, interviews, rock video techniques and music in TV wrestling shows. All the WCCW stars had their own theme song. The Freebirds entered the ring to Lynyrd Skynyrd's "Free Bird" until they recorded their own song, "Badstreet USA" (featuring Michael Hayes on the vocals). Gorgeous Jimmy Garvin's song was ZZ Top's "Sharp Dressed Man," Iceman King Parsons had "We Are Family" by Sister Sledge and my theme song became Quiet Riot's "Bang Your Head." The Von Erichs had a bunch of entry songs, I guess because there were so many of them: Kevin's was "Strangle Hold" by Ted Nugent, David's "La Grange" by ZZ Top, and Rush's "Tom Sawyer" for Kerry (his nickname The Modern Day Warrior came from the opening line of that song) and there are probably others I've forgotten.

Another element that made WCCW stand out was that it had revived the practice of using wrestler valets. Valets went way, way back in professional wrestling — everyone remembers Gorgeous George's valets — but they had been out of fashion for a long time. When I was there the star valets were Sunshine and Precious. Sunshine had started out as a heel — she was Gorgeous Jimmy Garvin's original valet — then he brought in Precious (who was his real-life wife, and they are still married!) and during one memorable match when Garvin wrestled Cowboy Johnny Mantell for the TV title and lost, he blamed Sunshine for his loss when it was really Precious' fault — and fired her. Sunshine then turned face and went with Gentleman Chris Adams to help create a major feud. John Mantell says to this day people still tell him they remember that match, so that shows you what a draw the valets were. Other valets came along later: Sunshine's "aunt," Stella Mae French the lady trucker and Nicola Roberts (Jake "The Snake" Roberts' sister-in-law and, more notably, promoter Nick Roberts' daughter, also called Andrea The Lady Giant and Baby Doll), but Sunshine was always the crowd favorite.

The Texas women valets weren't really wrestlers, even though women wrestlers had been hugely popular in the '50s and '60s. I was on many early shows where The Fabulous Moolah had her crew of women wrestling on a steady basis, but as time went on promoters just stopped using women to wrestle and they were even banned in a lot of territories. WCCW's female valets served two basic purposes: eye candy, because they were beautiful blondes in skimpy clothes (which attracted a lot of guys who weren't necessarily hard-core wrestling fans but enjoyed looking at the girls), and creating suspense around the outcome of the matches by interfering on behalf of their wrestlers. Since they were women, the men couldn't take revenge on them the way they could with male managers, and that would allow the bookers to keep feuds and angles going longer. Sometimes the World Class valets would be given matches of their own, but it wasn't what I would call wrestling, it was more like "cat-fighting" — slapping, hair-pulling, ripping each other's clothes — stuff to get all the guys going.

The Missing Link debuted in WCCW on Thanksgiving Day, 1983 at Reunion Arena in Dallas. This was a great way to be introduced to the new territory, because it was one of the most exciting shows World Class had put on that year. I wrestled in the second match with Freebird Buddy Roberts, who I beat easily. I beat him enough times when he was a Hollywood Blonde too, so it was just like the old days. I remember interfering in my first match that night too. I happened to be passing by the wings while another match was going on — Junkyard Dog was about to beat The Super Destroyers and Skandor Akbar said to me, "Go and knock him off." Akbar did not like The Junkyard Dog. So I ran the distance to the ring through the back crowd, climbed the post and turnbuckles until I was standing on the top turnbuckle, and with no hesitation at all, dove across almost the whole length of the ring and placed a head butt in the back of Junkyard Dog's neck, thus ending the match with a disqualification. Fritz saw me perform that dive for the first time in the ring that night, and afterwards I heard he called me "an athlete."

Kevin Von Erich took out Terry Gordy on the same card and David beat my soon-to-be tag partner, Kamala, by disqualification and held onto his Texas title. Mike Von Erich also made his debut at the same show, beating General Skandor Akbar — with a lot of help from Skandor. Remember what I said about the heel being the one who leads the match? Mike was a lot smaller than his brothers and always needed a lot of guidance to get through a match. The highlight of the show, however, was Kerry Von Erich beating Freebird Michael Hayes in a "loser leaves town" cage match, which had the crowd going wild.

WCCW picked up on the "mystery man" theme and started to promote The Link in the Mid-South. This is a typical write-up from one of WCCW's programs:

> *WHO, WHERE AND WHAT IS THE MISSING LINK? With no manager to talk for him it is very difficult to find out anything about The Missing Link. He is the strangest looking thing that has ever been seen in professional sports. What makes it even more mystifying is the fact that he has a magnificent body to accompany the goon head. Could it be that he is some former great that has flipped out? No one seems to know.*

Then when they started teaming me up with Kamala, we became General Akbar's two "junglemen." Kamala (James Harris) was an intimidating presence in his own right. He was a lot bigger than me: about 6' 6" and close to 400 pounds, and he always had his face and body painted like a tribal warrior, wore a loincloth and sometimes carried a spear. Kamala started as Sugar Bear Harris in Mississippi in the late '70s, went to England for a while, then started the Kamala gimmick in Jerry Lawler's Memphis territory. He went to Mid-South just at the right time and the gimmick caught on big there. I mainly remember how solid he was. Later on when The Link turned face and I would head butt Kamala in the chest it was like banging my head against a brick wall.

One wrestler I was really excited to be working with in Texas was Bruiser Brody (Frank Goodish). Back when I was based in Toronto, I remember Steve Bolus coming back from a tour and telling us he had never seen anything as large and as wild as Bruiser Brody. It was the kind of story that left you in awe; you'd think, *what was I going to see when I met him?* He was 6'5" tall with a 320-pound body, and had probably 15 years wrestling under his belt by the time I got there. He used his body the same way as Mick Foley would later, hurling himself at opponents, nonstop action, breaking furniture, sometimes carrying a long chain and participating in everything from cage to lumberjack matches. Although he had been trained properly on how to protect himself, he got many injuries — which showed, but he never complained about them.

My best memory of Bruiser Brody up to that point was the time I saw him wrestle Ric Flair to an hour draw in Kansas City, and in Texas I now had my chance to work with him. We were partners sometimes and opponents at others. I knew as his opponent I'd have to pull out all the stops and keep on top of him as much as I could. I remember one match when Bruiser hit me so hard with a chair I felt like my feet were sinking into the ring floor. I think he was just letting me know where I stood — I might think I was having a good run in World Class, but I wasn't to get above him. When I was his partner, I had to work equally as hard to shine or I knew he would outshine me. Bruiser is sadly missed now, probably by the fans too, but more so by many of the wrestlers who knew him.

* * *

As usual, I left it to my wife to make all the living arrangements for the move to Texas. She tracked down an old friend from our first stay in Shreveport who was now living in Denton, Texas, about 40 miles north of Dallas and found a brand new townhouse for rent right in Denton while she was staying with them. She and my son drove back to Bossier City to pack up everything yet again and arranged for a friend to drive it all out in a U-Haul. I was staying on another week to finish up in Mid-South, so she left a map for me and left a couple of days later.

When I got there, I wasn't too happy with the place. It was a new neighborhood, there was a lot of construction going on around it, and we had a cement alley instead of a backyard in the rear of the house. My wife said it was the best she could do under the circumstances but as usual I didn't think for a second about all the work she'd had to put into finding it. *I* didn't like it, and that's all that mattered.

I got back into the full swing of working, and continued my post-show partying, getting drunk and smoking a lot of marijuana. Not surprisingly, I continued having car accidents after shows too — three more. One night I got home about four hours late from a show in Dallas — wandered in drunk, stoned and half-asleep while my wife had been waiting up for me and worrying — and told her I thought I had hit something on the way home before I passed out in bed. In the morning, we both went out to look at the car and the driver's side was all smashed in. By this time I was able to dredge up a memory of hitting the side of the bridge on Interstate 35 on the way home. Did this narrow escape convince me that I should lay off the marijuana and alcohol for my own good? No, of course not. I decided my wife should take me to shows from then on since it was too dangerous for me to be driving alone. Instead of taking responsibility for my actions, I went into complete denial and dumped the responsibility on my wife. She went along with it, like always, reasoning that since our son had a job now, she didn't need to be at home as much.

So she did what I wanted yet again, and her reward was being treated like a hostage. She was always an uneasy driver, and she didn't know her way around Texas very well. The first time she drove me to the Sportatorium, she wasn't sure which exit to take and I flipped out on her, shouting and swearing, which of course upset her even more. I did apologize for blowing up at her after the show, blaming pre-match nerves, but it happened again and again and again. She'd tell me not to take it out on her or she wouldn't drive me anymore, but it was the same every time.

Then I decided if she was going to be at the matches as my driver, she should become part of the act too. Kamala had his handler Friday, so she could be The Link's handler, Sheena. We decided she would be dressed all in black too: skin-tight pants from Frederick's of Hollywood, a black silk blouse and black chauffeur's cap. I also made her a rhinestone necklace and bracelet. My wife was still a very good-looking woman and she looked great in the full outfit. We added some refinements — it was too hot in Texas to wear trousers all the time, so sometimes she wore black stockings and black shorts. I think she did enjoy being included in the gimmick, but she never got paid for any of her work — I never thought to ask anyone to pay her — which became a major resentment for her later on. Plus, I'm sure you can see what else was going on here. I was gradually getting her more and more under my control. With her driving me everywhere I was free to drink as much alcohol and smoke as much pot as I wanted after a match. On the way home from shows I would make her stop first so I could buy a six- or 12-pack of beer, a bottle of wine and fried chicken to eat on the way. When I was through eating I'd fall asleep and she would have to keep driving for three, four, or even five hours more. She started spending a lot of time talking to truckers on the CB radio to stay awake. They started calling her "The Lady in Black" and she became very well-known. I think this was actually good for her in a way. She was very bashful in person, so she loved being able to talk to people without any awkwardness, and they kept her company on the long drives.

Next, I decided I'd had enough of the townhouse and wanted to live in a trailer instead. I found a used one for sale in Fort Worth for $13,000 with a kitchen, bathroom, big bedroom and a pull-out couch in the living room for our son and bought it. The next step was finding a trailer camp to live in. I had heard about a nudist camp in Decauter, 20 miles west of Denton and we went to check it out. I should probably explain something here. We had gone to nudist camps in Ontario in the '60s when the boys were very young. Then it was a very cheap way to live and it was actually a good environment for kids. There weren't any singles, it was all families, and everybody was an equal once they'd taken off their clothes in the parking lot. You didn't know what anybody's job or social status was once you were in the park and everyone had gotten undressed, and we all called each other by our first names. The Decauter park was on 60 acres of beautiful parkland and the people were very friendly, so we made plans to move the trailer in as soon as it was paid for. It took another four weeks to pay off the trailer, then we told the townhouse owners we had been moved out of town and gave away all the furniture that wouldn't fit in the trailer.

We got lots of help from the other people in the park the day we moved in, and were invited to a dance being held on site that evening. I had to do a show that night, but I figured we might get back by midnight and could still go to the dance. The show went well, and we stopped off to buy beer and liquor on the way back, as we had been warned the camp was in a dry county so the camp clubhouse didn't have a bar.

We got to the dance and it became immediately apparent that this was a different kind of camp that the ones we had gone to before. Before, when there was a camp dance, everyone dressed up to the nines in their best clothes. Here, everyone was either naked or in really skimpy underwear. My wife was shocked and upset, because she realized right away that this was a "swingers" nudist camp — which meant wife-swapping, among other things. She grabbed my arm and said "What the hell have we joined?" She still had her all-black Sheena costume on from the show, so she really stood out in the crowd. I told her to calm down, and then started getting drunk. When she got up to go to the bathroom I took all my clothes off too and sent her off to get towels for a swim when she told me to put my pants back on. After a hot tub and a swim we went back to the trailer and I was asleep and snoring within two minutes. That was it. We never discussed the nature of the camp lifestyle again. I think she enjoyed living in the park aside from the sex and drugs scene, but her happiness was no longer my concern. What mattered is that I was happy there — there were lots of available women, liquor, marijuana and parties and if my behavior was hurting her, I didn't want to hear about it.

* * *

The death of 25-year-old David Von Erich on February 10, 1984 was a terrible shock to everyone in World Class. David was about to start a major tour of Japan but died in his hotel room the night he arrived. He was far and away the most talented wrestler of all the Von Erich boys and everyone was sure it was only a matter of time before David became NWA World Champion. The Link wrestled David the night before he left for Japan, neither of us knowing it would be his last match. I had been thrown out of the ring, which was on a stage in a large theater. Outside the ring I found a long ladder, which I placed in the orchestra pit and saw that it reached all the way up to the top rope of the ring, so I used it to climb back up into the ring, another classic Link antic that made this match especially memorable. The official cause of

David's death was a ruptured intestine, but there were rumors of an accidental overdose of tranquilizers combined with alcohol. I don't think it matters now. Whatever the cause, it was a dreadful loss for everyone. From then on in Texas, a sense that someone was missing never went away.

Fritz, however, turned this very personal tragedy into a triumph several months later, on May 9, 1984, when the first annual David Von Erich Memorial Parade of Champions was held in Texas Stadium in front of about 43,000 people, the largest crowd to ever watch a live wrestling show in Texas. The gate for that show was over $400,000, which was unheard of in pre-*WrestleMania* times. I had a short but exciting match at that show with Junkyard Dog (all the matches that day were short because it was so hot — it must have been about 125 degrees down in the ring) which I won, but was then disqualified due to Skandor's interference — he held onto the Dog's leg while I pinned him. That's the way a lot of my matches went. I lost very few matches as The Link, but often my wins were taken away because of something Skandor did. There was also a very exciting Freebirds-Von Erichs Six-Man Tag Title match that they wrestled wearing street clothes, which featured Fritz jumping into the ring with Kevin and Mike, whipping Michael Hayes with his belt, then holding off both Michael and Terry Gordy with an Iron Claw on each while Kevin pinned Buddy Roberts for the win.

The main event for that show was an NWA World Heavyweight Title match between Kerry Von Erich and Ric Flair, which was highly anticipated by everyone, fans and wrestlers. Fritz had never won the NWA World Title himself and he really wanted it for one of his sons — and until his untimely passing David had been the most likely candidate — so there was a lot riding on Kerry's shoulders that day. Kerry also had the memory of losing his chance at the title in Christmas 1982, when Terry Gordy knocked him out with the cage door to spur him on. It was a short match but fast-paced, and Kerry kept on top of Flair the whole time, matching him move for move. The crowd went absolutely crazy when Kerry reversed Flair's backslide with one of his own and pinned Flair to win the match. People threw yellow roses into the ring in memory of David.

★ ★ ★

Towards the end of 1984 things were getting slow again, so Fritz arranged for me to go to Eddie Graham's territory in Florida starting in January. Michael Hayes had left the WWF after a very brief stay, and was booking for Florida now, and Buddy Roberts was going there too. I had an elimination "loser leaves town" tag match on Christmas Day 1984 to prepare for my exit from WCCW. It was me, Skandor and "Mr. X" against Terry Gordy, Buddy Roberts and Chick Donovan. Obviously, we lost. The main event was another World Heavyweight Title match between Kerry Von Erich and Ric Flair (Ric had won the title back from Kerry about three weeks after the Parade of Champions). I actually worked one more match in Fort Worth on New Year's Eve against Terry Gordy, but it wasn't a main event. We started packing up the trailer and getting ready for the long drive to Florida.

I want to talk a bit now about character defects. This is something I didn't learn about until much later, when I went into recovery, but this next story is a good example of how abusing marijuana and alcohol was damaging my character. I've already told you how I started mistreating my wife, and this time my son was the victim. Not long after we moved to Texas I had found a vintage 1969 lime green Cadillac in the parking lot at a Denton mall I just had to have. You know me and Cadillacs by now. It was in perfect condition and had a For Sale sign on it, so I waited for the owner to finish his shopping and followed him home. He was asking $3,000, which I didn't have right then but we worked out a deal where I'd make weekly payments and allowed him keep the ownership until it was paid off. I made the arrangements and gave my old gray Cadillac (full of dents from all the accidents I'd had) to my son Jason so he could drive back and forth from his construction job in Denton. He spent about $1,500 of his own money to put in a new motor and fix it up.

However, there was also a young couple with three kids at the camp who I was quite friendly with and they needed a car so the husband could take a job he'd been offered. I knew they were quite poor and he really needed the job but this doesn't excuse what I did. I sold my son's car to them for *one dollar* — after he'd done all that work on it himself — in one of my fits of alcohol-and-marijuana-induced extravagance. I still can't believe I was so self-centered that I didn't think of how much that would hurt my son, but that's what the alcohol and marijuana brought out in me. I have a list of character defects I talk about when I do public speaking about addiction, and the elements they have in common is they're all side effects of addiction and all rooted in selfishness: impatience, intolerance, lack of consideration, egotism, self-righteousness, self-pity, laziness, enviousness, greed, spite, anger, hate, resentment, irresponsibility, promiscuity, unreliability, belligerence, defensiveness and vulgarity. Quite a list, isn't it? This particular incident was born out of lack of consideration, irresponsibility and egotism. My son needed a car to get to his job too, that's why I gave to him in the first place. But my out-of-control ego made me think that giving extravagant gifts to people I'd only known a few months was more important than the feelings of the people closest to me.

* * *

When we got to Florida in January of 1985 we moved into another nudist camp, mainly because it was a less expensive way to live. The atmosphere at this camp was a lot more wholesome than the one in Texas. There were mostly Canadians living there — very friendly people, and the setting was beautiful. It was in a town north of Tampa called Land O'Lakes and had a mobile home area, townhouses and big beautiful homes, a huge clubhouse with an outdoor bar, pool, tennis courts and hot tub. It was almost like being home, but with better weather. Within an hour of moving in, we met three other couples from Hamilton we knew from a camp in Puslinch, Ontario.

The next day, January 15th, we had to go to the airport to pick up my new manager, Percy Pringle III and get some publicity photos taken. This was Percy's unofficial arrival in the territory. He was just getting back into wrestling after a long break he took to finish school and get his mortician's license, so Michael Hayes (who knew Percy from way back) and the other booker, Dirty Dutch Mantell, had been priming the fans for Percy's arrival for weeks. The next day they had a live broadcast all set up at the airport. Percy was supposed to arrive by Learjet, and go straight to a live TV show at The Tampa Sportatorium. The Pretty Young Things were standing by at the airport with a limousine and between every match announcer Gordon Solie would check via satellite to see if Percy's plane had arrived. About halfway through the show Percy's plane finally landed — not a Learjet but a junky old Cessna propeller airplane, and Rick Rude appeared out of the co-pilot's door to tell the PYTs Percy's Learjet had been pulled for an overdue inspection and the old Cessna was the only plane available to fly him here. Rick and the PYTs pulled Percy out of the plane butt-first and fuming, and everyone piled into the limo to go to the Sportatorium for Percy's official debut in Championship Wrestling from Florida.

The original Pringle Dynasty was The Link, Ravishing Rick Rude, and The PYTs. Eventually Jack Hart, Rip Oliver, The Grappler, Jesse Barr and The Assassin joined. Some of the other wrestlers in Florida when I was there were Mr. "B" Brian Blair, Krusher Khruschev, Pistol Pez Whatley, Wild Bill Irwin, The Youngbloods, Terry Gordy, Bugsy McGraw, Wahoo McDaniel, and The Masked Assassins. I didn't make a lot of money working in Florida, but I sure had a good time. The weather was great, Percy was a lot of fun to be around and became like a part of the family in no time, all of us driving back and forth from matches in my big green Cadillac. However, it didn't take long for a tragedy to strike in the new territory too. On January 20th, Super Bowl Sunday, Eddie Graham shot himself. Eddie's son Mike was at the game and had to be paged to hear the terrible news. Everyone was shocked. Eddie had been in the business nearly 40 years and was highly regarded as both a wrestler and a promoter. He was NWA president for a few years in the 1970s and received many awards for his extensive civic and charitable work in the state of Florida, but I guess he had a lot of personal demons and they finally got the better of him.

After a few months in Florida, I went backstage after one of the Tampa shows — I think I wrestled Bugsy McGraw that night — and word came down that there were a couple of guys from *Sports Illustrated* waiting in my dressing room. Security cleared the room of the usual crowd of fans and hangers-on, and I entered in character, with "Sheena" leading me. As it turned out, *Sports Illustrated* was planning a cover story on the sudden boom in popularity of professional wrestling, and they wanted a picture of The Link to go with the story. I did my famous "hair-grab and roar" pose that so many fans had seen and they snapped away.

Even though they called wrestling "the original sham-sport" and the story was mostly about the WWF, the *Sports Illustrated* story was a sign that pro wrestling was moving away for good from its fringe roots into the cultural mainstream. They had pictures of a lot of people with the story: Kamala, Captain Lou Albano, Roddy Piper, Sergeant Slaughter, The Wild Samoans, Wendy

Richter and Leilani Kai, but The Missing Link took up two pages in the centerfold. The week after that issue was on the newsstands, the phone rang in our trailer at Land O' Lakes. It was George Scott, who was now booking for New York. He said, "Do you want to come and wrestle for the WWF?"

CHAPTER NINE

New York, New York

Going to the WWF in the spring of 1985 should have been the pinnacle of my career. Flush from the success of the first *WrestleMania*, Vince McMahon Jr. was scouting all the regional territories for fresh talent for the WWF. Many other star wrestlers from different territories were getting offers from Vince as he began building his empire, including some of the other top WCCW and Mid-South stars.

This was not my first experience with the New York territory, I had wrestled many times for Vince Sr. going back to my early career. Here's a little scoop about Vince Sr. — who used to show up at Madison Square Garden in a tuxedo — that I bet nobody's heard. He would open his books at any time and show you what everyone else was getting paid if you asked him. That was very unusual. But then, the New York territory had always been something of a world unto itself. The original World Wide Wrestling Federation (WWWF) started in 1963 when Vince Sr. and Toots Mondt decided to break off from the NWA so they could have their own World Champion and hold all the title matches at Madison Square Garden. When Buddy Rogers lost the NWA World Championship Title to Lou Thesz in January of '63, Vince and Toots refused to recognize the loss and announced a few months later that Rogers had won the WWWF World Title from Antonio Rocca at a tournament in Rio de Janeiro. This tournament never took place, but it paved the way for Bruno Sammartino to take the new WWWF Title from Buddy on May 17, 1963. The match was over in 48 seconds, which could have caused a big fuss back when fans were accustomed to World Title matches that could go on for an hour, but the crowd loved it because Rogers was such a heel that people were delighted to see him get taken out so fast by a newcomer.

The real reason that match was so short was Buddy Rogers had a heart attack only three weeks earlier. He refused to cancel the match and showed up at Madison Square Garden in a wheelchair, only getting up to enter the ring and be beaten in less than a minute. It was risky, because if people were disappointed by the first big title match the new promotion could have sunk real fast. But Vince Sr. knew he'd get away with it because he had such a huge following on the East Coast, where there are so many people and so many ethnic groups who would support his wrestlers — and all the Italians loved Bruno Sammartino, of course. Bruno held the WWWF Title on two occasions for more than 11 years and defended it against top heels all over the eastern territory — Killer Kowalski, Gene Kiniski, Dr. Big Bill Miller, and many others.

I had known Vince Jr. before too. I used to run into him at the gym a lot in the late '70s when I was wrestling in New York. He was really into the bodybuilder look — tall, great physique, big shoulders and trapezius, and he's maintained it very well. When I went into the office to meet with him in 1985 the first thing I said was, "Are you still working out?" He answered, "Oh, yes!" Even before he took over from his dad I had the impression Vince was a frustrated wrestler, which makes watching what he's doing now interesting. I'd almost call Vince a wrestling mark — I know he couldn't really be a mark coming from his background, but he believed in it the same way the dedicated fans did. They knew the matches were *worked* (predetermined) but they'd play along and get caught up in it all the same. I'm sure young Vince stood in the hallways and in the wings and watched how his dad did things, counting the days until he could take over, because he had his own ideas about how he wanted to run the shows. When he did buy the promotion from his ailing father the timing was perfect, because he had pay-TV and syndication deals, he had all the money he'd been left by his father, and a territory that would never go down because of the number of people on the East Coast.

I don't think there were too many of the old-school guys still around at the beginning of the modern WWF. Some of them had treated Vince like the coffee boy when his father was still in charge, and when he finally took over, those people were either long gone or they left very quickly. Certainly by the time I got there they were gone. If you're waiting for me to dish the dirt on Vince here I'm afraid you'll be disappointed, because I don't really have any. He treated me very well during the short time I was in the WWF, and I made a bad decision when I left. I knew the Vince behind the façade that he puts on TV, and I always found him to be very low-key and very much of a gentleman, just like his father. The enjoyment he seems to get out of being part of the shows now, making faces and acting out the part of a heel — I think it just proves my initial feeling that he wanted to be a wrestler all along. I've watched Vince work and he doesn't know any wrestling moves. He knows how to get knocked down and that's about as far as it goes, and I've never seen or heard of any promoter bringing in the whole family or exploiting sex the way he does either. I'm not sure how I feel about that. It's one thing if the family's all wrestlers, but to bring your daughter out and say she's done this, or ran off with that guy, or having the son and daughter calling each other names and fighting with their parents on TV? But then, Vince is their boss and he's the one who decides what ends up on his programing. I know he has scruples and there's a good side to him, but I guess when you're trying to make yourself number one, you have to bend the rules and act the part you've written for yourself. He's certainly a great leader.

I saw a TV interview once where his son Shane called Vince a "king." I wouldn't call him a king, but I saw another interview where Vince answered the question "What are you?" with "I am an entrepreneur." He's definitely the king of entrepreneurs and that's what I give Vince credit for: he had a vision and he went after it very successfully. So I wish him well, because he works very hard. It doesn't take eight hours a day to do what he does, it takes a lot longer, and he's made wrestling #1. If wrestling was #1 when I first started I would have been very happy, because we had to listen to people call us phonies, boo us and things like that. Now wrestlers are celebrities because of Vince's influence.

Vince's expansion strategy was essentially the same as WCCW's and what Jim Crockett was doing in Atlanta with TBS, incorporating entertainment elements like flashy costumes and rock music and using pay-per-view and syndication to extend the territory's reach. Vince, however, took it to a whole other level by actually offering TV stations in other territories cash payments to carry his shows instead of the ones from the local promoter. Nobody had ever done anything like that before and it must have cost him a fortune, but Vince had deep pockets and it helped him build a national distribution network very quickly by forcing out the local competition. The funny thing is, a lot of the smaller promoters dismissed the threat from Vince's expansion strategy at first because they figured he'd eventually run out of money with the way he was throwing it around.

The way I see it, the reason Vince and the WWF eventually triumphed is that he thought bigger than everybody else. Most promoters — Fritz Von Erich and Verne Gagne are good examples — couldn't really see beyond the boundaries of their own territory. Vince had grown up around wrestling and knew the business inside out, but he also had a university degree in business administration, and he knew there was far more money to be made by taking the WWF worldwide.

Besides taking away their television coverage, Vince also weakened the regional promotions even further by poaching all their top talent, and most of the stars didn't have to be asked twice to join the WWF. Again, it was mainly about (what else?) the money. If you went to a wrestling town in the WWF you got a $200 per diem for that night (and sometimes there would be three shows a night), then you'd get your regular check at the end of the week. I was making around $5,000–$6,000 per week, which was pretty high up on the payroll then. The WWF flew wrestlers to all their bookings, which meant I could go on living in Florida and they'd fly me to wherever I had to wrestle. When I signed my contract with the WWF I also got a small advance payment of $100 against anticipated sales of Link merchandise, which was something else no one had thought of doing before. Vince made lucrative merchandising deals for wrestler dolls, posters, T-shirts and lunchboxes and paid royalties to the wrestlers whose images appeared on them — which I didn't stick around long enough to collect on. A few months after I walked out, The Junkyard Dog told one of my sons he'd just got a royalty check for $250,000 from the WWF. No wrestler had ever made that kind of money before, even the main-eventers. You're going to hear me say a few times what a big mistake I made leaving so soon.

The Missing Link's official debut in the WWF was on the *Tuesday Night Titans* show. Bobby "The Brain" Heenan, my manager, took Vince (still playing the innocent, wide-eyed announcer in a bright red blazer) down to the "cave" where he claimed to have found The Link. This cave was the largest set Vince had ever built for a single wrestler. It had rocklike walls and a large entrance with a big fire pit in the middle, cooking a skinned rabbit for me to pick up and eat. I was in the back of the cave out of view of the cameras and when Heenan called out to me I trudged in, growling, and both Bobby and Vince had to shuffle around to make room for me. Vince interviewed Bobby while I walked around with The Link's distinctive slow, aggressive gait. When Vince tried to interview me next I backed away from the microphone roaring, grabbed my hair and ran back into the cave.

Despite all this build-up, right from the start I was a bad fit for the WWF, and that was mostly my fault. First of all they didn't want Sheena, just The Link. Vince thought they had enough husband-and-wife teams already. But since I was a non-speaking character, the gimmick needed a manager so I was paired with Bobby Heenan, and we didn't have the smoothest relationship. I don't blame Bobby for this either — again, it was just a case of a poor fit. When you're at the top of your game in wrestling, it's not always because a promoter told you how to get there. If you know your own strengths and talents, you can get yourself there and by that time you know how to handle your particular abilities in the ring. I had known Bobby Heenan a really long time, had watched him in the days when he was still wrestling, and he later became a manager for a number of top performers, but he wasn't that big a name when I first knew him. He had been well-known within the AWA but it wasn't until he got on with the WWF he became a nationally recognized household name.

So I think you can see the situation shaping up here. I was coming into the WWF from Texas and Florida where I made a star out of myself while Heenan was in New York making a star out of himself, and he was now a senior guy in the WWF making a lot of money. I can remember him saying to me, "All I care about is making my $90,000 a year and going home," which was fine, and good luck to him. But when I went to the WWF I felt like I was approaching the peak of my rise as The Missing Link. Then once I started working there it felt like that rise was stalled, because it became clear to me right away that nobody in the WWF really knew what The Link did, including Bobby. He just didn't understand how The Link gimmick worked and it ended up causing a lot of friction between us. Bobby had his style and I had mine and they did not mesh. We'd be doing a match together and I'd say to Bobby "do this" or "do that," because I was used to calling my own matches and I think that hurt his feelings, as though I was trying to order him around. I wasn't, because I had a lot of respect for him, but that was how I was accustomed to working as The Link. Bobby also had no patience with my expectation that he'd arrange all my plane tickets and deal with all the administrative details the way my wife did so I wouldn't have to break The Link's silence. His attitude was that he was my manager for the time we were in the ring and otherwise I was on my own. I don't remember ever getting angry or upset with him, but I think he got fed up with me pretty quickly.

When I say I felt like my rise was being stalled it doesn't mean I was ignored, if that's what you're thinking. The Link appeared on the cover of the WWF's "Wrestling Album" that came out that year, standing on top of a piano and here's another little scoop: Sheena was standing beside me when the original photo was taken. They took her out of the final version that appeared on the album cover. The Link also got a brief close-up in the video they made for the version of "Land of 1000 Dances" that was on the album. The Link wrestled mostly preliminary matches, against guys like S.D. Jones, Tony Garea, Aldo Marino, George Wells, Rick McGraw, Sal Bellomo, Jose Luis Rivera, Lanny Poffo, and Swede Hanson, but I also had some memorable main-event bouts during my months in the WWF. I fought George "The Animal" Steele, Brian Blair, Ivan Putski, and Tito Santana, who I wrestled several times for the Intercontinental Heavyweight belt but never won. I think it would have been interesting if they had put a title on The Link, but it didn't happen for me in the time I was there.

I wasn't any more recognizable as Dewey Robertson to my old friends in the WWF than I had been in Mid-South or World Class. The day Iron Mike Sharpe Jr., my young protégé from Dewey's Gym (who always claimed to be Canada's #1 athlete when he was in the WWF) came into the dressing room with Bill "Masked Superstar" Eadie (whom I'd also known for years) and saw me sitting there for the first time, they both walked to the other end of the room. Normally, wrestlers shake hands with everyone in the dressing room, but I must have been quite a sight at 260 pounds and in full makeup, so neither of them made a move towards me. After two weeks working with Mike and other guys I'd known before, I finally "outed" myself as Dewey Robertson, just as I had done with Buddy Roberts. They were stunned. They really didn't know it was me until I told them. Other people who were still in Canada saw me on TV and later said, "I thought it might be you, but it was really hard to tell."

I started to get recognized as The Link a lot after joining the WWF and I always tried to put my best foot forward. I used to wear a cap to cover my bizarre haircut when I was out in public until the day I was walking in downtown Denver, Colorado with Nikolai Volkoff and Mr. Fuji. We spotted a group of young people, one with spiked hair and the others with different punk haircuts. They were across a big downtown square but within eyesight. Nikolai and Fuji said to me right away, "Take your hat off." I took my hat off and the kid with the spiky hair noticed immediately and beckoned me to come over. We had a good laugh and I kept on walking, and from then on I never wore a hat again.

Another time I was sitting in the New Jersey airport waiting for a flight when two cops spotted me from about 500 feet away. I was at my peak weight of 260, very muscular, and wearing my customary all-black traveling ensemble: black golf or polo shirt with all the identifying labels ripped off, black pants, black thongs and The Link goatee and haircut. The cops didn't recognize me as a wrestler, and must have thought I was a biker or a member of some bizarre gang. They came over and started asking questions and in keeping with The Link persona, I responded to their questions not with words but low groans while my eyes wandered slowly, never making contact. My thought was: they could ask me for ID at any time and that would end my little act, but they never did. They finally gave up, but as they walked away, I heard one say to the other, "There must really be something wrong with him." If they'd only known!

* * *

I was really looking forward to one WWF match on July 24, 1985 at Buffalo's Memorial Auditorium, because for the first time in my career, I was booked to wrestle André The Giant one-on-one in the main event. I had never had a singles match with André — they were always Battle Royal-type matches with many participants. The WWF was selling out Buffalo Auditorium continually, and they had recently raised the roof on it to accommodate more fans, so the place was packed to the rafters. Unfortunately André was double-booked somewhere else in Europe and couldn't make the match, so the WWF substituted their former heavyweight champ and my old mentor, Bruno Sammartino. Bruno had lost a few pounds, but was still suffering from the extremely bad back that he had developed from his long run as the world champion. I could see right away what kind of pain he was in and knew that body-slamming Bruno or taking the match to the wild side would be unfair. I also had so much respect for him for being the champion for so long, and for giving me my first break in the business by booking me in Pittsburgh that I said to myself: *This match has to go his way.*

At that time during arena shows they would have boxing and wrestling commissioners sitting on three sides of the ring, in high-back chairs with narrow tables in front of them to write the results on. The men in the chairs were long-time commissioners, and each was probably at least 70 years. (In case anyone's still wondering, the main reason Vince eventually went to sports entertainment as opposed to professional wrestling is that it helped him get rid of all the commissions and the fees he had to pay them.) The tables were still in good condition but I could see the wood had been worn very thin on the tops and I knew they were very old. So I, in the interests of saving Bruno from any further physical damage, did the unthinkable. During the first few minutes of the match I didn't even get in the ring where Bruno was waiting for me. I ran around doing Link antics, growling at people, banging tables and chairs on my head, the usual stuff. Then I ran around the ring again, and one by one I smashed in the top of each commissioner's table with one short head butt. That alone would be enough to put any wrestler or boxer out of the business for good.

Somewhere in the back of my mind I knew the only thing I could do to keep from being barred from wrestling after a stunt like that would be to put Bruno over. At about the four-minute mark I jumped to the apron and flew between the ropes, but as I went through I caught my foot deliberately on the bottom rope and got myself hooked between them. Bruno was there and pinned me very quickly for the 1-2-3, which made everybody very happy, including the commissioners. And the noise from the crowd — well, I thought the new roof would blow right off the building. But that was a very stupid risk I took. I think I had more speed and marijuana in me that night than any other time I wrestled, and since I never got a chance to talk over what I wanted to do with the promoter or with Bruno before the match (and they would have talked me out of it, I'm sure) I probably came as close as I ever have to ending my career completely.

As time went on, I began to build up a lot of resentment over the way I was being treated by the WWF. I didn't like being separated from my wife so much, and I didn't like the way they kept shuffling managers on me either — for a while it was Johnny Valiant, and sometimes Captain Lou Albano did TV interviews for me too. That was OK. I had known Lou Albano in Pittsburgh when he was starting out as a "fall guy" like me, and we had gotten along well because we were both learning the business from the bottom up. Lou went on to great success tagging with Tony Altimore as The Sicilians, a terrific mobster gimmick, then became one of New York's longest-running heel managers.

Sometime in the fall of 1985 Heenan traded The Link to Jimmy Hart, The Mouth of The South, who had come up to New York from the Memphis territory a few months before I arrived and was managing King Kong Bundy and Greg Valentine. Heenan got King Kong Bundy in exchange for The Link and Jimmy Hart became my manager. I left the WWF a few weeks after the trade. I didn't have any hard feelings against Jimmy for what happened. I had even talked to him about feeling unhappy with where my career was going, so he understood it wasn't his fault when I left. It was the $50,000 bounty match with Mr. Wonderful Paul Orndorff at Boston Gardens that finally did it for me.

The old Boston Gardens was always packed for shows, especially down the aisles. The narrow lead in to the ring was so close that people could touch their favorite wrestlers or abuse the ones they didn't like. When Blackjack Mulligan left the ring after beating Pedro Morales, he got an injury from a fan that required 165 stitches in one leg. Paul Orndorff had a superbly muscled, well-conditioned body from his football career (luckily, he'd sustained no major injuries) and quickly turned into a great wrestler. He had such intense speed that he could hardly stand still, and this became a disadvantage for him during our match. Paul didn't know The Link never started from a referee's starting lock-up position or made any eye contact during the match, so that left him not knowing what to do as the match started.

Jimmy Hart was running around the ring wearing a flaming fuchsia pink jacket and shirt with a black tie and yelling instructions at me with a megaphone. As he made a noisy gesture Paul took his eyes off me to look at Jimmy and The Link charged to take an advantage that lasted about six minutes, which was usually about all the time it took for The Link to handle most opponents. Paul endured the body-slams and head butts knocking him all over the ring until the tables turned, when Jimmy got up on the apron and started hollering at The Link to finish him off. The megaphone got very close to my ear and triggered a mood swing which caused me to turn on Jimmy in anger and take my eyes off Paul. Paul slowly got up from the canvas and took the opportunity to charge me with a high-flying knee between the shoulder blades, knocking me into Jimmy and knocking Jimmy right off the apron. I was forced backward another step as Orndorff slid beneath me for a simple roll-up onto the shoulders, and 1-2-3, the match was over.

When I got up, both Hart and Orndorff were gone. As I left the building after the show my thoughts were going crazy with fury at losing the match, because The Missing Link had only been beaten four or five times in eight years (Orndorff, Bruno Sammartino, and two of the Von Erichs), being handed over from manager to manager, the company insisting my wife stay at home in Tampa, and all these resentments, fueled by addiction, finally boiled over into action. I went straight to the airport after the match and slept on the floor all night next to a bag lady who watched my luggage for me, waiting for a flight to take me home to Tampa.

The shame and remorse over making that decision to walk out of the WWF is something I'll never forget. Not necessarily because I would have made a lot of money if I'd stayed, but because it's one of the worst career decisions I made due to my addictions. If I had been thinking straight — pun intended — I might have looked at things more logically. If anything was the right time and place for me it was in the WWF then, but addiction kept me from seeing that. I was stuck on that feeling of being stalled, even though something else told me that maybe Vince was just putting me on the side to hold off for a while, like he did with The Rock early in his career. The Rock was put aside and then when the time was right for him, he got the push as a heel and went right to the top. Looking back now, that might have been what Vince was planning for me, but because I was on marijuana and alcohol all the time I was becoming more arrogant and difficult to get along with, and it seemed like everything else in my life was spinning out of control too, and so I didn't pay attention to those second thoughts. And it's not like people didn't try to steer me right. After I left, George Scott, the booker, called and pleaded with me to return. "Please come back," he said, "you could retire here." I honestly believe that I could have stayed ten years in the WWF if I had been in my right mind, but I don't know if I could have turned around my addiction to drugs and alcohol during that time either. You don't look ahead and say, "Well, now I'm making good money, so I'm going to stop drinking." Whatever your circumstances are, good or bad, the addictions will carry on and eventually destroy you if you don't do something about them.

Anyway, that was the end of my run in the WWF. I went back to Texas where I was more comfortable (with the money about to start going down, down, down) and more importantly, where there was nothing to interfere with my use of alcohol and marijuana.

★ ★ ★

Nobody thought much of it when I returned to World Class from the WWF. Plenty of other people from Texas had gone to New York and not stayed very long. The Freebirds had an even shorter run in the WWF than me, and it wasn't because they didn't get over well. They had the same experience I did, of the bookers there not understanding how the gimmick worked and feeling like they didn't fit in. The final straw for The Freebirds in the WWF was a decision to split them up. Terry Gordy left to go to Japan and Michael and Buddy took The Freebirds to the AWA for a very successful run with Jimmy Garvin in Terry's place. Plus, World Class was still formidable competition to the WWF at the time. WCCW's TV shows actually had higher Nielsen ratings than the WWF's all through 1984 and 1985. Under Ken Mantell's guidance, the World Class TV shows had gone from being seen in 35 markets to 159. People in Boston, Philadelphia, Chicago, California and many other places who were used to seeing a more predictable kind of punch-kick wrestling went crazy for the Von Erichs and all the other World Class characters. Want another scoop? Both Vince McMahon Sr. and Jr. had come down to Texas in the early 1980s to meet with Fritz and proposed that the WWF and WCCW join forces and go international. Unfortunately (though nobody knew then just how unfortunate it was), Fritz declined. He said to them, "Why do we need you?" World Class could have been big, but in the end Fritz just didn't have that kind of vision. Ken Mantell had the opportunity to book shows outside the territory three or four times a week, in all these new places where people were starving to see the World Class wrestlers, but Fritz wouldn't let him.

My wife and sons left Tampa and we all moved into another nudist camp called the Ponderosa, near a small town in Texas called Wills Point. My two sons were now training to be wrestlers too — my older son had left his first marriage and was back living with us. They began tagging at smaller shows as The Sterling Brothers. Mark was as tall as me, but lankier — he never built his body up to the point I had. My younger son Jason was more muscular, with a tiny waist and big legs but much shorter than either of us — he was only 5'8" and maybe 180 pounds, though they'd always announce him as 210 in the ring. I think he might have done well in Mexico or Japan if he'd had the chance, because he was an acrobatic, high-energy flyer. Boy could he zip around that ring, and he sure loved the attention of the fans.

I know Jason genuinely enjoyed being a wrestler, but Mark I'm not so sure about. To this day I really don't know if he really wanted to do it or just started training to please me. I think Mark saw the downside of a wrestler's life more clearly than Jason: the abuses, the animosity and particularly the financial hardship. I think about this a lot, because I have a very difficult relationship now with my son Mark and it causes me a lot of pain and regret. For a very long time he didn't speak to me at all, then we had a short truce and he stopped again. I believe he's carrying a lot of anger over the things that happened during this period of our lives but he won't tell me exactly what, he just says I should know what I did that made him so angry. I've come to the realization that I can't force him to forgive me, all I can do is pray that one day that he will be ready to tell me all his resentments so we can clear them up and maybe start fresh.

* * *

When I starting wrestling for World Class again in late 1985, Fritz decided it was time for The Link to do a face turn. He saw that I was as popular as any of their babyfaces, plus they had a whole new collection of heels. Gary Hart was back managing One Man Gang, Chris Adams had turned heel and teamed with Gino Hernandez and as The Dynamic Duo they were feuding with the Von Erichs and newcomers Hollywood John Tatum and Missy Hyatt were creating lots of havoc. The Pringle Dynasty had also jumped to World Class, with Percy managing Ravishing Rick Rude and causing mayhem as only Percy could. Percy even got his own column in the World Class programs where he cheerfully insulted both the faces and the fans week after week. "To you people who attend our matches and scream your fool heads off for Neanderthals like the Von Erichs, neither my magnificent wrestler nor I mind your 'boos.'" World Class also needed to bump up their face side a bit. There was a new Von Erich, Lance, who was allegedly a cousin of the brothers, but he wasn't really a Von Erich (he wasn't even an Adkisson). I went back to being managed by Percy for the time being as they set up The Link's face turn. They revived a rumor from before I left that The Link had a crush on Sunshine, so my face turn began one night when The Link was supposed to wrestle Michael Hayes. The match started with Hayes in the corner abusing Sunshine and The Link going into a rage, chasing him away from her and throwing him out of the ring, then picking up Sunshine to lift her into the ring to safety. This was a bit of a challenge: I had to shift my shoulders and change my grip a little to get her over the top rope, which put her lovely round butt smack in my face. Sunshine didn't flinch a bit from being in this undignified position. She was always one-hundred-percent professional when we were working. She was The Face — she always had the right expression for whatever the situation was, without even trying.

The big change went down at the 1985 Christmas night show,

which was typically when new angles for the coming year were set up. That was a great show, featuring The Freebirds making a triumphant return to World Class and rekindling their feud with the Von Erichs. I pinned Jack Victory in a mid-card match, then my big moment came when Sunshine "rescued" me from Percy and Rick Rude and declared herself my new manager. Her massive popularity gave credibility to The Link's face turn. After Christmas a backstory about The Link began to emerge, to bolster this dramatic change in character. Somebody cooked up a sad tale about The Link's previous life as an abused foster child who imagined he was a wild beast to cope, and ran away to join the freak show of a traveling carnival, where Skandor Akbar found him, taught him to wrestle and then handed him on to Percy Pringle. With the help of Sunshine, aided by Ken Mantell and Fritz Von Erich, they were slowly rehabilitating The Link and helping him remember that he was a man, not an animal. It was great stuff, and they ran it in the WCCW wrestling programs immediately following the Christmas match.

For my part, I enjoyed having Sunshine as my manager — not only was she a seasoned professional in the ring, she was the most perfect, beautiful, wonderful person outside it too, always smiling and happy. I really loved her. Everyone loved her. I hope she'll resurface one day, I would very much like to see her again. One interesting thing that happened after my face turn is that The Link became very popular with children. The kids seemed to understand that The Link, like any other beast, had a "kitten" side and they were drawn to it. I had one solo match with Buddy Roberts where he went and grabbed a teddy bear away from a little girl in the audience (for a while it was trendy to use dolls and toys as props) because he was annoyed at the way the match was going. The Link had been charging and head butting him nonstop, and Buddy ran out of the ring because he was scared to stay in there any longer. Buddy stomped around outside gesturing and complaining to the referee, then grabbed the teddy bear in frustration and jumped back in as the crowd booed and yelled. The Link stopped in front of him and stared, then moved slowly to stare at the little girl, then back at Buddy. All of a sudden The Link charged Buddy again with three deadly head butts that knocked him right out. I picked up the stuffed bear, slowly left the ring and walked over to the little girl. The place went absolutely silent, because no one was sure what The Link would do. People were on the edge of their seats as I silently handed the little girl her bear. A spontaneous "Awwwwww," erupted from the crowd. After that match, The Link started getting hundreds of teddy bears in the mail and I'd be inundated with them whenever I entered an arena.

As a result of my new popularity as a face, Fritz basically ordered me to start signing fan autographs, which I had not done as a heel. That's one of those old unwritten rules, heels don't sign autographs. I argued this was against the whole concept of The Link character being non-communicating, but Fritz told me I was going to do it whether I liked it or not, so I had to figure out a unique way for The Link to sign autographs. After a lot of thought I came up with the idea to sign it backwards, as though I had just recently learned to write. I would start with the "K" and go right to left to spell out "Link." I still didn't talk though — that was left to Sheena, my wife, who accompanied me everywhere again. The fans would give the pictures or whatever they wanted signed to her and she'd give them to me. I also started visiting children's hospitals dressed as The Missing Link. I've always had a good rapport with children, maybe because I'm still a big kid myself in a lot of ways, and I still have folders full of children's letters and photographs from then.

So while on the surface everything seemed back to normal, there was trouble brewing on several fronts, both within World Class and the wrestling world in general. I don't think Fritz or the promotion ever really recovered from the death of David Von Erich and now some of the other boys were starting to have problems. In the summer of 1985, while I was wrestling in New York, Mike Von Erich suffered a shoulder injury during a match in Tel Aviv. Post-surgery complications left him physically weak and mentally unstable. I'm not sure Mike was ever meant to be a wrestler but he kept on pushing himself, trying to keep up with his brothers. Then Gino Hernandez died in February 1986 from a massive cocaine overdose. What was really ironic was that he and Chris Adams had just split up The Dynamic Duo and set up an angle where Chris was "blinded" by having hair-removal cream rubbed in his eyes by Gino after a grudge match between them. This was being hyped as a big tragedy, and then Gino died for real a few days later. I told you earlier I wasn't going to point fingers at anyone's behavior but mine and I meant it, so all I'm going to say about the manner of Gino's passing is that Texas was not a good place for people with drug and alcohol addictions to be, including me. It's right on the southern border where a lot of illegal drugs enter the U.S., and the culture in World Class didn't exactly encourage abstinence. I'm not saying any more than that, but it's no secret that most of the Texas wrestlers were a hard-partying bunch, and by 1986 it was starting to catch up to us.

And as if Gino's death wasn't enough of a shock, a month or so later Bill Watts really threw Texas for a loop.

CHAPTER TEN

Mr. Universal

It had always been a sore point with Bill Watts that Mid-South Wrestling was considered a second-tier promotion next to the Big Three: the AWA, the NWA, and the WWF. Bill's irritation with that attitude was understandable, as he was possibly one of the best promoters ever (and I think the most obvious proof of that was that the WWF kept stealing his talent). Bill knew that a good wrestling show was more than just a main event, and his TV shows reflected that philosophy — they were a running serial, like a soap opera, that kept people tuning in week after week to see what would happen next. There would also be weekly title defenses to keep the interest high, and entertaining commentary by Watts and referee-turned-announcer Jim Ross. When I see Jim Ross on TV now, I think back to when he refereed in Tri-State for Leroy McGuirk, and as Dewey Robertson I tore his referee's shirt off I don't know how many times. I also have a photo of Jim standing beside The Missing Link holding his hair on the back of his head.

As 1986 began, two of Mid-South's most popular wrestlers, Junkyard Dog and Hacksaw Butch Reed, left to work for New York, and Bill Watts began making his own expansion plans. The success of the Mid-South TV shows had given Bill the idea that he really could compete with the Big Three, and he decided to start building his own nationwide syndicated television network. He also thought the promotion needed a new name to match these exalted ambitions. In March of 1986 Bill announced that Mid-South had a new name: The Universal Wrestling Federation. He renamed his TV show *Bill Watts Presents . . . The Universal Wrestling Federation*, and moved the production unit to Tulsa.

Bill also went on a Vince McMahon-style talent raid in Dallas. He hired Ken Mantell away to be his booker, and most of the top talent in World Class left with Ken. Skandor Akbar and Devastation Inc., John Tatum and Missy Hyatt, One Man Gang, Chris Adams, the Freebirds, Sunshine, Iceman King Parsons and The Missing Link all joined the UWF. I think the reason so many people left World Class, even though Bill Watts was a lot tougher to work for than Fritz (like I said before — Bill paid well, but boy, did you earn it) was Bill treated all his talent more or less equally whereas Fritz was obsessed with putting his sons over at the expense of everybody else. Bill was also offering people one-year contracts instead of paying on the house like Fritz did.

Bill's move probably came at the worst possible time for World Class. Fritz had just withdrawn from the NWA — which left him free to put whatever titles he wanted on his boys, but meant that he lost the Ric Flair World Title matches and the credibility those matches brought to the promotion — then there was the sudden loss of Gino Hernandez, who was a top heel. And while the spring 1986 Parade of Champions had drawn a decent crowd of around 24,000 with all kinds of exciting matches — Sunshine and Missy Hyatt in a mudpit match, Bruiser Brody pinning Terry Gordy in a barbed wire match, a tag match with The Link and Iceman King Parsons against Skandor Akbar and One Man Gang (that we won when Iceman pinned Skandor) and a lumberjack strap match for the Six Man Tag Title pitting Steve Simpson, Kerry and Lance Von Erich against the Freebirds — right after that everyone left for the UWF and suddenly Fritz had no more star attractions. Fritz was furious at this betrayal and threatened to sue Bill after a UWF/NWA card in Dallas drew more than his July 4 Independence Day Star Wars card (which actually drew a perfectly respectable 11,500 people). Bill responded to this by creating a second TV show, *Power Pro Wrestling*, and taping it at the famous Billy Bob's honky-tonk in Fort Worth, right in the heart of World Class. The gloves were off, as they say.

Even before the raid on World Class, the UWF's roster of talent was very solid. Bill had faces Hacksaw Jim Duggan, Steve "Dr. Death" Williams, Ted DiBiase, Terry Taylor, Brett Sawyer, Chavo Guerrero Sr. and The Fantastics, and heels Jake Roberts, Eddie Gilbert, Buzz Sawyer, Dick Murdoch, Dick Slater, The Blade Runners (featuring a very young Sting and Ultimate Warrior), and The Sheepherders. When I got to the UWF Bill gave me a new manager, Dark Journey. She had been Dick Slater's manager first as a heel, but turned face when she was put with me. Dark Journey was a strikingly beautiful girl — tall and slim, she was from a mixed racial background so she had an exotic look that fit in well with my "from parts unknown" gimmick. She also made a good visual contrast to the blonde valets like Missy Hyatt and Sunshine. Other than that I don't remember a whole lot about Dark Journey, to be honest. She was always kind of a loner and I was too wrapped up in my own ego to pay much attention to her when we weren't working together. The Link character continued to develop. I stayed a babyface, and gradually The Link evolved into a loveable goon who could be counted on to provide comic relief rather than the fearsome Neanderthal I was at first.

Bill hit the ground running with all his newly acquired talent, first reviving an old Georgia feud that pitted The Freebirds — who now had Sunshine as their valet and The Angel of Death as a "bodyguard" — against Ted DiBiase and Dr. Death. Bill even came out of retirement to challenge Eddie Gilbert's "Russian Invasion" — Eddie, Krusher Kruschev (Barry Darsow) and Korstia Korchenko — himself. It sounds a little silly now, but 1986 was the height of the Reagan Era when the Cold War was still taken very seriously, and they drew huge heat for that feud.

When I went back to Texas from New York, even with all the bad habits I had, my wrestling kept getting better and better. And many times when I had matches against top wrestlers, they would ask me, "What do I do?" before a match with The Link. I would always say to them, "Just meet me in the ring and everything will go fine." Then afterwards they would come up and congratulate me, and say things like, "Gee, that was such an easy match." Just ask Terry Taylor. He reminded me of a number of wrestlers I had met in the later part of my career, usually younger guys, who always wanted to know before the match what we would do in the ring. Chuckling to myself, I'd look at the concern on their faces and recalled my own younger self, asking the same questions whenever I was faced with wrestling someone older that I didn't know very well. I always repeated what the older guys had said to me: "We'll see what comes up in the ring."

The Link got a lot of solo matches with Buddy Roberts, who was approaching his career peak as I was approaching mine. It was a great opportunity for Buddy to step into the spotlight, because now Michael Hayes and Terry Gordy both had enough experience that they didn't need his help as much in the ring. I consider Buddy Roberts to be a true icon of wrestling, from the time I first wrestled him in Montreal when he was Dale Roberts, to our feud in Tri-State when he was one of The Hollywood Blondes and our incredible one-and-a-half hour match, to helping create one of wrestling's greatest tag teams, The Fabulous Freebirds. Buddy and I were so used to working with each other that whenever we had a match together in the UWF it was what wrestlers call *a night off*, meaning smooth sailing all the way.

Bill created a UWF World Heavyweight Championship belt to go with the new name and held an inaugural tournament in Houston on May 30, 1986 in front of a sell-out crowd. I wasn't a contender for the belt, but most of the promotion's top names were in it: Chavo Guerrero, Buzz and Brett Sawyer, Jack Victory, Blade Runners Sting and Rock, Kamala, Rick Steiner, Terry Taylor, Koko B. Ware, all three Freebirds, Hacksaw Duggan (who had held the old Mid-South North American Title before the name change), Ted DiBiase and Steve Williams. It was Terry Gordy's night to shine as he downed one opponent after another: Koko Ware, Ted DiBiase, Dr. Death, to the championship final against Hacksaw Duggan. Duggan was the favorite to win the new belt because he'd held the old one, but before the final match One Man Gang attacked him and slammed Duggan's head into the bolts that attached the turnbuckle hooks to the ringposts, causing him to start bleeding uncontrollably. (This was a real injury that eventually became infected.) Duggan bravely went ahead with the title match but he was too weak to put up much of a fight and Terry Gordy pinned him easily for the championship win.

★ ★ ★

At the beginning of 1987, the UWF had still had a strong roster of faces: Hacksaw Jim Duggan; Steve "Dr. Death" Williams; Ted DiBiase; The Fantastics; Chris Adams; The Missing Link; Terry Taylor. And heels: One Man Gang; Eddie Gilbert; and Missy Hyatt's Hot Stuff International, which now included future stars Sting and Rick Steiner; the latest version of Devastation, Inc.; Wild Bill Irwin; Eli the Eliminator and as always, The Freebirds (with the Angel of Death filling in for Terry Gordy, who was in Japan again). But the year began with a bad omen. Hacksaw Duggan, one of the most popular faces, was getting ready to leave for the WWF. He had been feuding with new UWF Heavyweight Champion One Man Gang, in a series of brutal cage and chain matches during late December and early January. On January 23, 1987, Duggan lost a "loser leaves the UWF" match to The Gang, setting up Hacksaw's departure. Duggan had also been tag team champion with Terry Taylor, so Bill declared the tag team titles vacant and held a Tag tournament, which took place on Saturday, February 7, 1987 in Fort Worth. I was teamed with Chavo Guerrero, Sr. against Rick Steiner and Sting in the first round, which we lost by disqualification. In the first match of the second round, Ted DiBiase and Steve Williams wrestled against Chris Adams and Iceman King Parsons in a face-vs.-face match, but Ted and Steve were attacked by Devastation Inc. instead. A fight continued outside the ring with Adams jumping out to assist DiBiase and Williams in fighting off the bad guys. Parsons stayed in the ring as the referee counted to ten, disqualifying Ted and Dr. Death and awarding the victory to Adams and Parsons because the Iceman stayed in the ring. Parsons argued that the team should accept the win and advance to the title bout but Adams refused. Bill Watts flipped a coin to solve the disagreement and said the winner could continue with a new partner. Adams won and invited Savannah Jack to team with him.

Iceman got his revenge by attacking Savannah Jack after his

singles match with Mike "The Hippie" Boyette, leaving Jack lying outside the ring and forcing Chris Adams to choose another partner. Adams chose the former defending champ, Terry Taylor. The championship match was the best of the night, with Adams and Taylor emerging victorious as new UWF Tag Team Champions.

In March there was another shakeup, this time on the heel side. The Angel of Death was supposed to wrestle Skandor Akbar's Ninja, but instead the Angel turned on Michael Hayes at ringside and he, Akbar and One Man Gang all attacked Hayes, adding more fuel to the fire of The Freebirds-Devastation rivalry. The Link was also feuding with The Freebirds (mostly Buddy Roberts) during this time, over my "crush" on Sunshine. Dark Journey was still my valet for the matches against Freebirds, but she and Sunshine never got a match together — Sunshine ended up facing Nicola Roberts, daughter-in-law of Grizzly Smith (she was married to Sam Houston, who was another one of Grizzly's sons).

By the end of March 1987, Terry Gordy was back from Japan so there were three Freebirds again, but Ted DiBiase, who was probably the top face after Duggan, left for a Japan tour around the same time. Bill had been trying to make deals with smaller promotions that didn't want to join the WWF or Jim Crockett Promotions (NWA Atlanta) but wasn't having much success. They resented being strong-armed, and Bill's "people skills" often left something to be desired. He had already permanently alienated Fritz Von Erich by stealing most of his best talent, then by taping the *Power Pro Wrestling* TV show right in the heart of World Class territory. Bill had even approached Verne Gagne about a partnership, but Verne turned him down because the AWA was slowly fading away too.

One thing I can say with confidence is that the UWF did not fail because we were putting out inferior product. Many people said and still say that Bill's TV shows were head and shoulders

Before wrestling, I loved to travel

In the '60s, wearing a Kiniski-type jacket while trying to become NWA World Champion in St. Louis

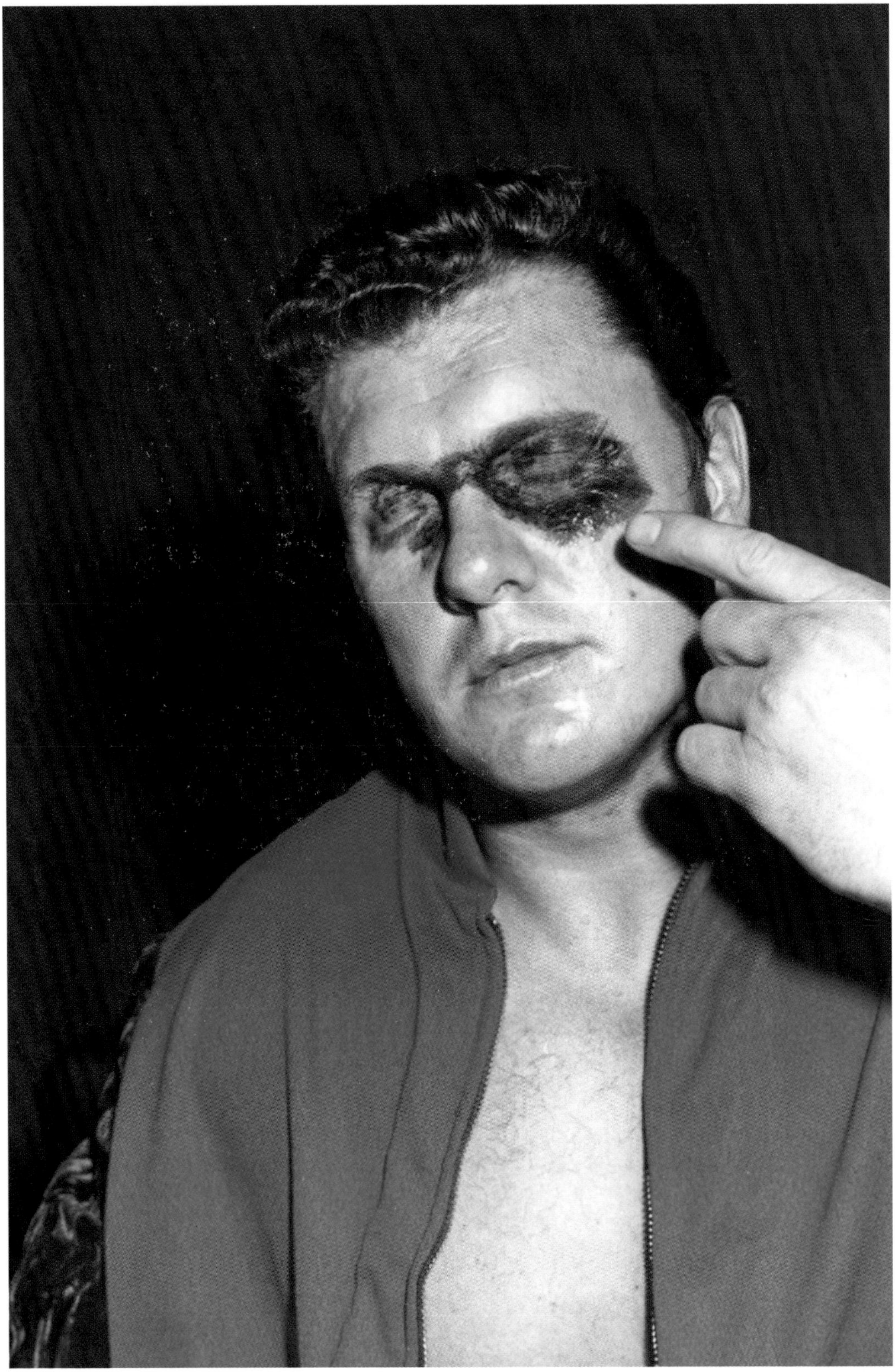

Louisiana, 1971: eye injuries have caused recurring bouts with temporary blindness

Fighting Bull Johnson, one of the men who trained me, in Toronto – the ref is Fred Atkins, a very important early mentor

George Wells, a great footballer and my tag partner – good times in Charlotte

Kansas City: my first successful heel run – just before leaving for Texas, shaving my head, and becoming The Link

Wrestling main eventer Dick “The Destroyer” Beyer

Buddy Rogers and me

My successful gym provided us with a house, serenity, and stability

Bigger and better: "10 years ahead of the times" with a new, modern gym

My gym opened in 1973 – President Reagan urged everyone to get fit in '83

Percy Pringle and The Link

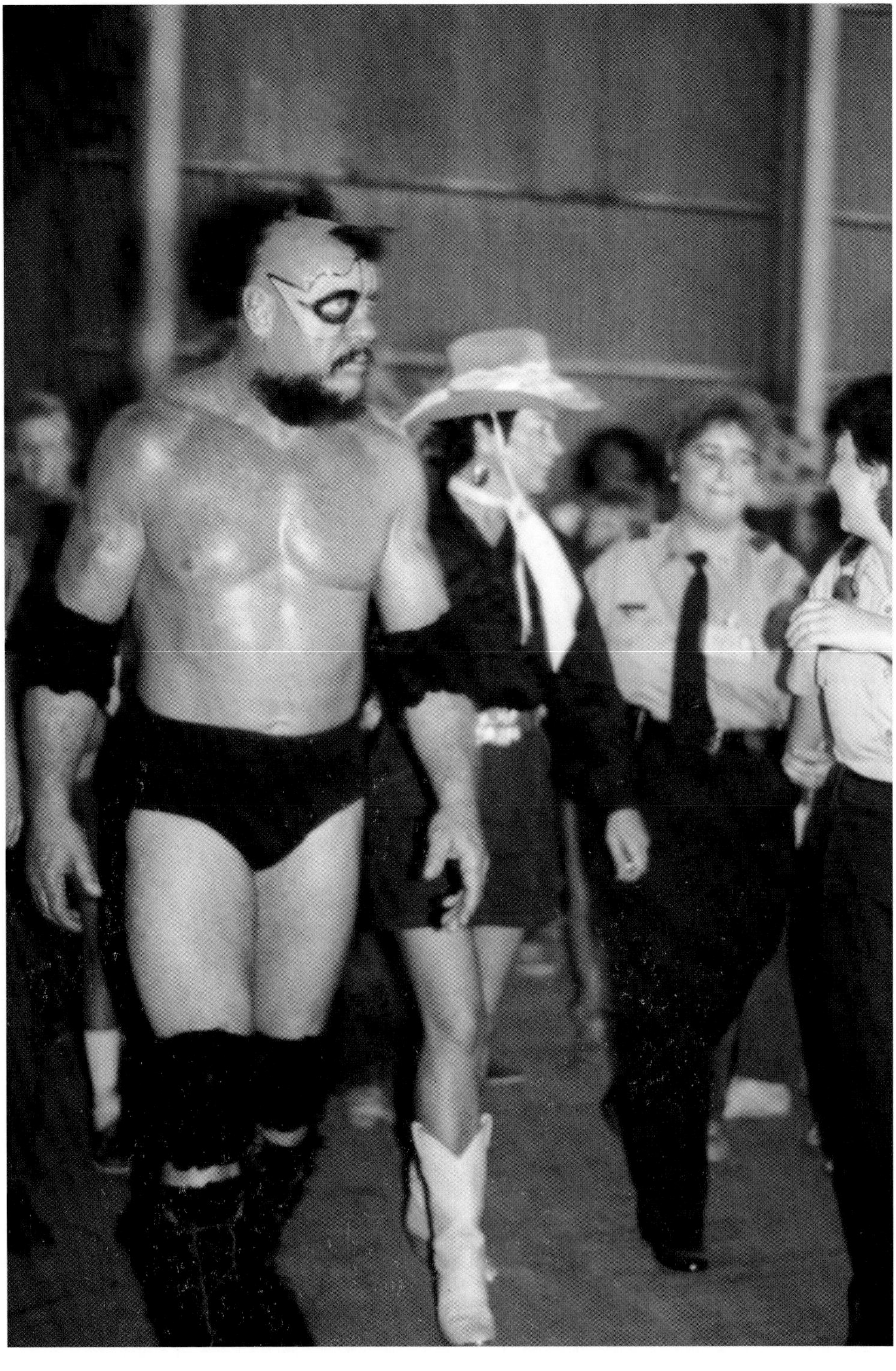

The Link and Sheena entering the Fort Worth stockyards
for a Boy Scout Jamboree – 10,000 strong

One of the first times I realized a background could help put me in character

The Link – out of character

Basking in the adoration of the crowd

On the set of *Maniac Mansion* – as "The Atomizer"

Me, Percy, and my son Jason – backstage, Copps Coliseum

The Link photographs Kerry Von Erich in Hawaii

Back home in Hamilton

My son Jason, following in his father's footsteps

Jason and The Link on an ESPN wrestling broadcast

To this day my connection with children is my greatest achievement

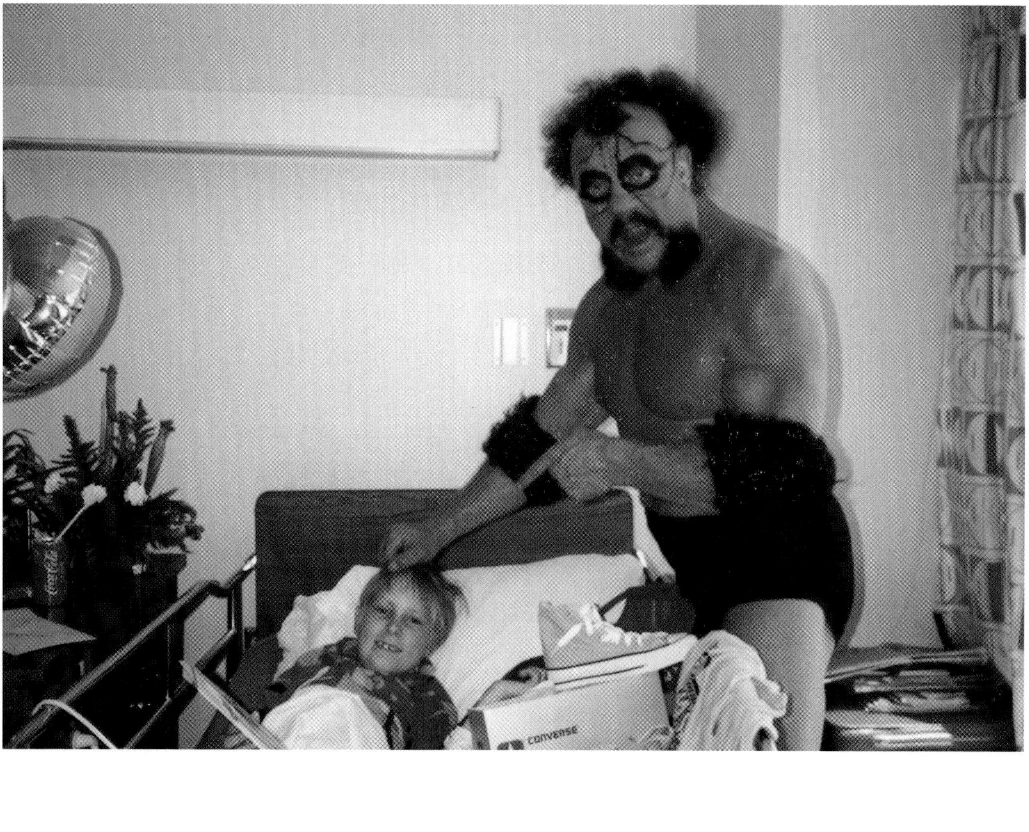

above the offerings from the WWF and NWA, which were strictly "enhancement" matches like the ones I had done so long ago in Pittsburgh. Bill had stars wrestling other stars, title changes, face and heel turns — the whole package week after week. But in spite of the quality of the wrestling shows he was putting on, Bill's expansion plans were not working out the way he'd envisioned. Some of that was due to his personal shortcomings, and some of it was circumstances. It's funny, a lot of people now seem to think it should have been very obvious by 1987 that Vince was going to triumph over the smaller promotions, but for those of us who were there at the time, the outcome was by no means certain. A lot of serious wrestling fans disliked the cartoony stuff coming out of New York (Houston promoter Paul Boesch once called Vince "the Walt Disney of wrestling").

I personally believe Bill Watts tried his best to make the UWF a national promotion, and could have succeeded if not for several big factors mostly beyond his control. Lack of money was the major one. Bill was a sharp businessman but he'd had to go too heavily into debt before he'd built up a solid national audience and achieved the kind of cable TV saturation that the WWF and Jim Crockett Promotions had. *Power Pro Wrestling* had a time slot on TBS, but it wasn't enough to compete with New York or Atlanta's programming. The UWF also didn't have the kind of massive local fan base New York and Georgia had to draw on. The UWF's main cities were in Texas and Oklahoma: Houston, Fort Worth, Oklahoma City and Tulsa, and the promotion would run a three-day swing on Saturday, Sunday and Monday every other week in these cities, taping the television program on those nights. The problem was, aside from Houston, none of these cities were big enough to pull in the kind of money at the gate he needed to finance a national expansion. Bill had tried expanding outside the UWF's core area by putting on a show in San Bernardino, California, but it flopped miserably, drawing a crowd of a few hundred. Bill thought he was going into uncharted territory but forgot that the Big Three had also been running arena shows on the West Coast for years. Despite Bill's best efforts, he remained limited mainly to syndicated shows within the five-state UWF base, which was large but sparsely populated compared to the Eastern Seaboard where Jim Crockett and the WWF were operating.

And while Bill always had superb talent working for him and was always very canny about getting good coverage in the wrestling magazines, he didn't have easy access to the New York-based national media and thus was never able to produce a wrestler with the kind of breakthrough mass appeal of the WWF's Hulk Hogan. Hulk had very limited wrestling skills, but a great look and tons of charisma, and he became a mainstream celebrity very quickly. Children worshipped Hulk. Even people who didn't follow wrestling or live anywhere near New York knew who he was. The UWF had plenty of people who could have become as big as Hulk — Junkyard Dog, Jake Roberts, Butch Reed, Ted DiBiase and Hacksaw Duggan were all hugely popular and charismatic main-eventers — but they kept leaving the promotion and taking their fans with them.

Bill had also made some questionable business decisions. Offering everybody contracts instead of paying on the house had cost him a lot. Moving the television show to Tulsa and Fort Worth was also very expensive. Going to Fort Worth had been a bold-faced attempt to undercut World Class, and that move plus the talent raid had pretty much sealed the coffin on any cooperation between Bill and Fritz Von Erich, who might have been able to help him out financially. Their working relationship had always been rocky anyway — when I first started in Texas Bill and Fritz were cooperating with each other, sharing their top wrestlers and sharing the benefits, but eventually they clashed over something (not surprising with two such strong personalities) and the relationship soured again. Also, Bill Watts was an Oklahoman and Fritz was a Texan, and I heard many times while I was in the South that Texans and Oklahomans just do not get along. Be that as it may, there was no question that World Class, already in a downward spiral after the deaths of David Von Erich and Gino Hernandez, was hit very hard by Bill's actions. But in the end it didn't do Bill a whole lot of good either — it just fragmented the Dallas market to the point were no one could make money. Bill also put the squeeze on the local promoters who ran individual towns within the territory, trying to get every last dime he could out of them and alienating a lot of them in the process.

And the one factor completely beyond anyone's control was an extended economic slump that hit all the oil-producing states where the UWF was based — Arkansas, Louisiana, Mississippi, Oklahoma and Texas — during 1986 and 1987, which meant a lot of the people who used to come to the house shows, which were still the promotion's bread and butter, couldn't afford to go anymore. By the beginning of April 1987 Bill Watts had no success finding backers, and was facing bankruptcy — he has claimed that he was losing up to $50,000 a week before he sold out. He was also going through a messy divorce at the same time (and I believe his ex-wife ended up getting all the Mid-South/UWF tapes as part of her settlement).

As a last-ditch effort to get his money back Bill tried to manipulate Vince McMahon into buying him out by threatening to file an anti-trust suit against the WWF, but Vince told him to take it to court, knowing Bill couldn't afford to wait out a lawsuit. Instead Bill got Jim Ross to call Jim Crockett Promotions in Atlanta and tell them McMahon was interested in buying the UWF, to push Crockett into making an offer. Jim Crockett had been biding his time, watching what was going on in Oklahoma during the previous year and waiting. He and Bill had tried co-promoting several shows in New Orleans earlier in the year, but

Jim chose to step back from any closer ties and basically waited for the UWF to go bankrupt. However, when he got the call from Ross he agreed to make a deal and in early April 1987 Bill sold Jim Crockett both the UWF name and the TV shows for somewhere in the neighborhood of $2.2 to $4 million, depending which reports you believe. Bill didn't say anything to the workers about the sale — not even to his son Joel, who produced the TV shows. Instead he let Jim Crockett break the news to everyone. Jim just showed up in the dressing room at a show in Monroe, Louisiana, and told everyone he was now the boss.

Bill had also neglected to tell Paul Boesch about the new arrangement, which didn't impress Paul too much as he had a major UWF show booked for the first of May. I don't know why Bill chose to alienate Paul that way, given their longstanding relationship and that he was probably Bill's most powerful ally in the area. Bill and Paul had a made a very profitable partnership in the early 1980s when Paul allowed Mid-South to supply the talent for Houston Wrestling, and for years the Houston Wrestling TV show was the top-rated show on UHF in the area. Paul had heard of a possible deal between Watts and Crockett but could not get answers from either of them when he tried to find out the details — so Paul took matters into his own hands by calling Jim Barnett at the WWF and making an offer. The May 1st UWF show was canceled and a couple of weeks later Channel 39 aired its first WWF tapes in place of the usual UWF show. After news of the deal got out, Bill called Paul up blustering about how as a shareholder in Houston Wrestling he should have been consulted, but Paul had been listening for months to other people complain about how Bill tried to railroad then, so he didn't budge, and the other stockholders eventually bought out Bill's share.

I didn't stay with the UWF after Bill sold out. Ken Mantell left soon after Crockett took over and found some private backers to start his own promotion called Wild West Wrestling, booking matches and running a training school at Billy Bob's. A lot of the UWF talent, including me, chose to go with Ken, because Jim Crockett's main concern at this point was empire-building — he was in direct competition with the WWF, and he had bought out the UWF mostly because he wanted the TV shows and the stations they ran on to add to his network. Jim opened a second office in Dallas and named the new company The Wrestling Network. At first he kept the UWF name, but since there were now a lot of duplicate titles and programs, he began merging them with the Atlanta programing. By the end of 1987, the UWF as a separate entity was gone.

CHAPTER ELEVEN

The Wild, Wild West

While Bill Watts had been struggling to keep the UWF afloat, World Class Championship Wrestling was quietly collapsing too. Fritz was still coping with the aftermath of the deaths of his son David and Gino Hernandez, and then in June of 1986 Kerry had the motorcycle accident that crushed his left foot and put him out of action for nearly a year. Kerry nearly lost his foot as a result of that accident and eventually had to have his ankle fused, which severely hindered his abilities when he did get back in the ring. Kerry soldiered on with the characteristic Von Erich determination, never letting the fans know the extent of his injury, but his wrestling was never the same again. And Mike had still not recovered completely from his 1985 shoulder injury and subsequent bout with toxic shock syndrome either. I don't want to dwell too much on the Von Erich family's personal problems, but they are part of the story of how the Texas territory eventually went under.

By the fall of 1986, the talent exodus plus the economic downturn in the oil states was hitting World Class very hard. The turnout for the Cotton Bowl card in October 1986 was only about 5,800, bringing in about $72,000 at the gate. The Christmas Star Wars 1986 turnout was disappointing too, with only 7,000 and just under $68,000 at the gate — it had been more than double that just two years earlier. And sadly, there was still more tragedy ahead for Fritz. Early one morning in April 1987, Mike Von Erich was pulled over for drunk driving and police found a collection of pills and marijuana in his car. Mike disappeared that afternoon, after the family's lawyer paid his bail, and was never seen alive again. He left a suicide note at his apartment and one in his abandoned car, and about a week later his body was found lying in a sleeping bag in the underbrush around Lewisville Lake, dead of a Placidyl overdose. He was only 23. Poor Mike. He was never going to be the wrestler his older brothers were, but he couldn't bring himself to disappoint his father. I guess trying finally wore him out.

Mike's death hit Fritz Von Erich very hard. Wrestling had been Fritz's life — he made it his sons' lives too and now it seemed to be taking them from him one by one. Mike's name was added to the 1987 Parade of Champions but the event only drew about 6,000 people, a far cry from the tens of thousands who packed Texas Stadium from 1984 through 1986. Kevin Von Erich was the current WCCW Champion, and then he collapsed a few days later during an eight-man tag match in Fort Worth. More than ever, there seemed to be a pall over the promotion. But Fritz wasn't about to give in without a fight. In May 1987 he hired a marketing company owned by his friend H.R. "Bum" Bright to revamp the TV show and plan a national tour for the promotion. Things picked up a bit in the summer of 1987 when 4,000 fans came out for a house show in Mesquite featuring new WCCW champion Al Perez, but attendance at the fall shows stayed stagnant and the much-touted Von Erichs Across America tour wasn't a huge success. Some of the cards drew well, but the rest were not very profitable.

Meanwhile, Fritz was also eyeing Ken Mantell's Wild West Wrestling, which was doing quite well. Ken set up a Wild West Tag Team Title tournament on November 30, 1987 with 14 teams. I teamed with Jeff Raitz and we made it to the final round and wrestled John Tatum and Jack Victory for the title, but they won. Jeff was an enthusiastic and creative young wrestler, hung around me a lot and worked out with me in the gym, but unfortunately he was trying to break in when things were going down. I just learned recently that Jeff died a few years ago at the age of 38. He was younger than I was when I became The Missing Link. So many people I knew are dead now and many of them younger than me. It gets hard for me think about sometimes. I hear about someone I knew who's gone and, even if I haven't seen them in a long time, I miss them. You travel with someone, wrestle them, get to know them well and when you hear they've passed on it makes you wonder why you're still here.

Towards the end of 1987 Fritz Von Erich finally threw in the towel and sold the promotion to Kerry, Kevin and Ken Mantell, who merged Wild West Wrestling into World Class. Ken got 40% and Kerry and Kevin 30% each, which meant for the Christmas Day Star Wars show World Class had some of their old stars back. I wrestled the show's first match against Vince Apollo (which I won), followed by my son Jason against The Real Thing (Rip Morgan). Fritz tried to give the Christmas Day card some punch by pretending he'd had a heart attack right before Kerry was going to wrestle WCCW champion Al Perez in a cage match for the title. They set it up by having Terry Gordy show up and say he wanted to challenge whoever won the match to a title defense, then Buddy Roberts, Iceman King Parsons and The Angel of Death stormed the ring to attack Fritz and Kerry. Fritz was waiting to be handcuffed to Gary Hart but ended up handcuffed to the cage and during the ensuing brawl Fritz got hit on the head by Iceman's famous "rooty poo" stick. Kerry and Kevin got Fritz out of the cage and then he collapsed onto the floor, clutching his chest. Eventually he was taken away by paramedics and Kerry announced that he was going to wrestle the next match anyway because that's what his father would want him to do. It wasn't necessarily intended to be another "Von Erich tragedy" but most of the fans thought it was genuine, so they just ran with it. I think that pretty much tells you what the atmosphere was like in World Class by that time.

★ ★ ★

Going into 1988 it still seemed possible that the promotion would rally and come out of the slump. Ken had his TV production machine in full gear and the show was on ESPN — The Freebirds, Chris Adams, The Link, Iceman King Parsons and Terry Taylor were all back in World Class, and my son Jason got booked for some matches against WCCW Light Heavyweight Champ Eric Embry (still as Jason Sterling). Because of the ESPN coverage we were seen around the world, and I got to go on one of the tours of Israel, where WCCW was hugely popular.

Dallas sent out 13 weeks worth of wrestling tapes that were shown in different countries in the Middle East to prepare for the tour. They had never seen American wrestling before and were captivated by the wild television antics. When the whole Wild West crew arrived we had to be guarded by a dozen soldiers at all times, to keep the friendly but enthusiastic crowds back. We wrestled in Tel Aviv the first night, and after the matches and a late dinner, a couple of officials took me around the city to meet all their relatives and friends, in different houses and apartment buildings. The crowd followed us most of the night, so I had to escape out the second story windows of each house. I was fed at every stop, and the journey lasted until nearly dawn. I remember falling asleep in the chair of my hotel room and waking up to see the sun rising over a body of water outside my window.

After that we went on to Haifa, where we wrestled for the next eight days. I shared a hotel room with Mark Romero, and from our 8th-floor window I could see clear across the city to the stadium. It was huge, most likely a soccer stadium, probably held about 50,000 people and it was full eight nights in a row. They had to have the soldiers running along beside the van when we arrived at the arena to get through the large crowds, because everybody wanted to get so close to the wrestlers. There were tin sheets in front of ringside that took a lot of abuse from The Link, as I used them to open up cuts all over my head.

The Israelis had never seen anything like The Link before. I asked them to take me to the beach one day when I was really tired and fell asleep while lying in the sun. When Valerie (Sunshine) came to get me for the show that night, there was a crowd of people gathered around me about five paces back and eight deep in a big circle, loads of people just watching me there sleeping on the sand. It was hilarious. I got some of the finest treatment of my career by the people in Israel. We were picked up at the hotel and driven to the stadium every night, and after the show they'd take all of us out for fine dining, first-class all the way. I expressed my gratitude by threatening to leave unless they got me something to smoke — which was an empty threat because they had my passport, but still. I'm afraid I wasn't much of an ambassador for pro wrestling.

Despite my increasingly erratic and egotistical behavior out of the ring, The Link continued to be in demand in other territories. Ken Mantell got The Link booked for a show in Memphis, and while we were there he decided to take his daughter to visit Graceland and invited me to come along. As we were waiting in line at the ticket booth across the street, people began to recognize me because of The Link's bizarre haircut and beard, and ask for autographs. To Ken this was a good strategy for selling tickets but it was a huge thrill to me, being recognized at the home of the King of rock 'n' roll. If you've never been to Graceland you should go for two reasons: to see how one man from tiny Tupelo, Mississippi, could capture the attention of the world, and also how addictions could destroy that same man. Addictions don't discriminate.

Ken also booked The Missing Link to wrestle Tuffy Truesdale's bear. It made sense, since The Link's persona was still a kind of beast-man, but I have to admit, Dewey Robertson was extremely nervous about facing a bear and wondered if I might wet my pants during the match — or worse. Earlier in my career I had seen Luis Martinez get his finger bitten off by a bear (who was muzzled during the match). Jim Conway was knocked out cold when a bear cuffed him, and I watched 12 wrestlers get chased into the dressing room at Detroit's Cobo Hall by a bear that got loose and ran out of the ring. I even pulled a little rib on Skandor Akbar in 1971 when he was booked to wrestle a bear. This was during my Tri-State run and Skandor vs. the bear was the main event of a show in Hot Springs, Arkansas. The bear was chained to a pole in the basement of the Civic Center, and about 20 minutes before the match I sneaked downstairs to agitate the bear. I thought that would be a good joke. Now that the shoe was on the other foot, I didn't think it was so funny.

Fortunately for me, by this time the Humane Society had forbidden wrestlers to have any actual contact with bears in the ring, so Ken told me how the match would go. "You go to the ring, where Tuffy will have the bear on a rope. As you get partway into the ring, he'll release the rope, and the bear will charge you." I did this about 10 times, then finally left the ring and ran back to the dressing room. The bear was declared the winner of the match. If you want me to tell you how it really feels to be charged by an angry bear, you'll have to come and see me speak in person.

Another time Kerry Von Erich and I were invited to do a one-nighter in Hawaii, because both Kerry and The Link were very popular there. Hawaii wanted us so badly they paid for the match two weeks ahead of time, which is *very* unusual in the wrestling business. I got $1,000 for the night and Kerry probably got more. Puerto Rico also wanted The Link — they had seen me on ESPN and called Ken Mantell to ask if I could come there and wrestle Stan "The Lariat" Hansen (he and Bruiser Brody were the two big American main eventers in Puerto Rico). I arrived very early with lots of time before the match, so I went down to the beach and found Stan Hansen there. I went over to introduce myself and say hello because I'd never met him before. Wrestlers generally like to look each other over before they wrestle for the first time, and I didn't find him much bigger than me, just heavier in weight. He didn't go to the gym much. Stan was a cowboy from Texas and was always armed with a steer rope (or lariat) and chaps in the ring, hence his nickname.

Once we were in the ring together Stan's style would be to jump me as the bell went, and he proceeded to do it, pinning me with big forearms. When it was time to introduce the head butt, I butted him in the chest. Stan was not a man to go off his feet too easily, but I began to knock him down. I hadn't gotten to Stan's head yet when he found a steel chair from somewhere and with that I began to take punishment on the back, and on the head. As you know, The Link never sold any kind of a reaction when getting hit on the head. This battle, which was being televised in three cities at the same time, went on back and forth for 10 minutes. The

Puerto Rican fans, judging from the noise in the crowd, were in awe. The burly Texan couldn't make a dent in The Missing Link. I felt bad at this point and pulled Stan into the corner, whispering to him "Would you like me to sell a little bit more?" by which I meant take a few bumps for him and make him look good. Being the nice man he is, Stan whispered back "What's the use?" knowing the match was a great brawl. Then we both went outside the ring, got disqualified and laughed about it afterwards. Stan was one of the great roughhouse wrestlers, and I haven't seen him since so I never had a chance to thank him for the great match. So thanks, Stan.

Things were not going very smoothly in the World Class office, however. Fritz had brought back Gary Hart to take over as booking agent and TV producer after Ken Mantell left, and once Ken was back at World Class gradually a power struggle grew between him and Gary, which just added to all the tensions already present due to the economic troubles in the territory. Gary and I didn't get along very well during this time either. I guess I must have formed some resentment against him out of the ongoing conflict with Ken, because I didn't know Gary very well before Texas and never had any other reason to dislike him.

For his part, Gary thought I was a discipline problem and an arrogant SOB (true on both counts). I was often rude to Bronko Lubich, the referee, asking him why he didn't retire, and Gary had to tell me to lay off on a couple of occasions. He didn't approve of my lifestyle either. Gary knew I lived in a nudist camp and that offended him, as did my promiscuous behavior, which got back to him via other people because I wasn't bothering to hide it as my addictions progressed. There were a couple of rather ugly incidents between us that I really wish had never happened, and because of that I feel I owe Gary Hart an apology. He was one of wrestling's greatest bookers and managers, one who could not only work successfully with gimmicks but also created them himself — The

Great Kabuki, One Man Gang — and I should have given him more respect. I should have given Bronko more respect too — he was kind enough to give me a bit of money when I had to leave the territory.

Gary wasn't Ken's only source of conflict during that time. He also had to contend with being partners with the Von Erich sons. Don't get me wrong, I loved all those boys but they were a handful to manage, and I don't think they really had the mindset to be bookers. When you're booking matches, you're not just thinking about next week, you're thinking about two months down the road. They were the promoter's sons and used to winning, so most of their ideas centered around which outside wrestlers were coming in that week to be beaten by the Von Erichs. Let's face it, that's going to get old eventually. Most people who were fans of the promotions Ken had booked — World Class, UWF and Wild West — liked them because the storylines weren't predictable and there were always surprises and twists in store every week. Besides having to navigate the backstage politics, Ken had a lot on his plate just trying to build World Class back up to what it had been: booking, supervising the TV shows and making sure all the World Class wrestlers showed up for their matches meant he was working 18-20 hours a day.

There may have been a lot of signals during this time that World Class/Wild West's days were numbered, but they were lost on me. I figured that since Ken had built The Link up to such a height of popularity that the good times would go on forever for me and I never, ever worried. Because of alcohol and marijuana, I never thought about the future. I was getting more and more withdrawn from reality in my personal life too. After living for awhile in the Ponderosa nudist camp, we rented a trailer on Lake Tawakoni, near a gym where I liked to work out. By this stage in my addiction I was a daily drinker and pot smoker. Within 10 minutes of getting out of bed I'd light up a joint, and I knew all the tricks, like smoking it in the shower to hide the smell. When I wasn't wrestling or working out I would sit in front of the TV watching The Missing Link promo tape Ken had made for me and drinking Wild Turkey bourbon on the rocks. If there were other people there, I'd make them watch the tape too and look at my centerfold in *Sports Illustrated.* Basically, I was living in a dream world.

I had bought a big red Dodge Power Ram truck and made it into a "Linkmobile," putting steer horns on the front of the hood with the help of a couple of local kids, and we would drive around to matches and public appearances in it. The Link's popularity continued in Texas, even as the payoffs were going down. I could cause a stir in the Wal-Mart parking lot by going into character. One time I was lifting weights in a friend's garage and a car went flying down the road past us, then hit the brakes and stopped, and two little girls got out and came running down the driveway with their autograph books. I immediately went into character again, pointing at a cow in a field and mooing, and those little girls' eyes got as big as saucers.

I had a lot of good ideas about how to promote myself as The Link, but with the territory declining and so much in my personal life being out of control I couldn't be realistic. One of my ideas was to build a Missing Link amusement park and I tried to get a local banker to lend me a large amount of money for it, but I had nothing but my truck to put up as collateral. Needless to say, I didn't get the loan. I was talking to people about going back to Canada and bringing down a wrestling ring to practice in and tour with — both my sons were in Texas with me and I thought we were all going to go on the road together, but I was not seeing what was in front of me. My son Mark, in particular, was getting very disillusioned with the business and with my behavior, and eventually left to go back to Florida where he'd had a good job.

I didn't take the hint.

★ ★ ★

In 1987 Fritz had begun trying to make inroads into south Texas, including Houston, where the World Class TV programs had always been quite popular. World Class continued to run cards in Houston until May 1988, when the "Triple Dome of Terror" show, featuring a return match between Kerry Von Erich and Iceman Parsons with Michael Hayes on the card, drew less than 100 people. That was it for Houston. The turnout for the 5th Parade of Champions May 8, 1988 wasn't much better than the previous year, about 7,000 people, even with two title matches on the card: WCCW Texas Tag Champs John Tatum and Jack Victory against Terry Gordy and Steve Simpson for the Wild West Tag Title; and Kerry Von Erich against Iceman King Parsons for the WCCW Title in the main event. Jason and I teamed against Vince Apollo and The Angel of Death in the first match on the card and won when The Link pinned Apollo. Jason also won a Triple Dome Texas Roundup match teaming with Steve Casey and John Tatum against 14 opponents, including The Angel of Death, Mike George, Terry Gordy, Michael Hayes, Iceman King Parsons, Buddy Roberts, Shaun Simpson, and Jack Victory. It was a great show, but far from the huge moneymakers of a few years previous.

It was heading into the summer of 1988 when things really began to fall apart for me. We had left Lake Tawakoni and moved into a townhouse in Mesquite when we went back to working for Dallas, then had to move into a not-very-nice hotel across the street from the house so we put our furniture in storage, along with all kinds of wrestling souvenirs: programs, videotapes, posters, everything. After a few months we went to pick everything up — Jeff Raitz came with us that day — and the guy who owned the storage facility took us to open the door. It was a huge locker and it had been packed so tight with stuff the door would barely shut. Now we looked inside and there was only a couple of boxes and one of our couches left. Everything else was gone. The guy was obviously anticipating our reaction, he had his dog with him and as we looked at him he made a motion like he was reaching for a gun, immediately on the defensive. "Don't do anything to me, I don't know what's going on." We found out later he had done this to other people previously, and that the "insurance papers" we had signed weren't really for insurance. The guy was also an Ecstasy dealer and a wrestling mark, and I'm sure he made a point of telling whoever he sold our furniture to that it used to belong to The Missing Link.

That was the beginning of the end for all of us in Texas. During the same period Jerry Jarrett from the Memphis territory was making overtures to the Von Erichs about forming an alliance with World Class and what was left of the AWA to co-promote shows in all three territories. I don't really know what happened behind the scenes because I was trying to keep my own life from falling apart, but the short version is that Ken lost his backers and Jerry Jarrett ended up buying World Class outright for a sum far below what it had been worth, eventually merging it into a new territory, the USWA. I would guess that Ken either got squeezed out in the deal or decided he didn't want to work for somebody else, having been burned several times already. I can remember Ken saying "Texas is hell" — at one point he had 35 countries lined up for tours and a database with thousands of names of people who wanted to train at his wrestling school, but the carpet got pulled out from under him yet again. I do know Ken left Texas and opened up a Wild West office in Ontario, California (he had wrestled in California a lot early in his career), and tried to carry on, but unfortunately for him, the time of the independent promoter was coming to an end and he had to shut down for good. That sealed Ken's disenchantment with the wrestling business and he has dropped out of sight entirely, which is a shame. I counted Ken as a good friend from the time I first met him on my early tour of

Louisiana, when he was still wrestling. I admired his wrestling style, and when I met him again he was invaluable in helping me create the gimmick that gave me another run as a star. The Missing Link was as much Ken's creation as mine, I want everyone to know that. All the wrestlers who worked with him respected his talent and creativity, his work ethic and his character. The wrestling business can easily change a good life to a bad one but it never did that to Ken. He was always a good person, very hard-working, devoted to his family, and committed to building a good wrestling company.

Ken had been sending some of the World Class talent up to Kansas City for matches — one night near the end of May I wrestled Bulldog Bob Brown and the main event was a tag match with Kerry Von Erich and Michael Hayes against Iceman King Parsons and Buddy Roberts — but the situation there had gotten even worse than it was when we left. A main event with Kerry Von Erich at Memorial Arena would be lucky to draw 300 people. My son had some bookings up there along with a few of the other Billy Bob's trainees, so we went up with him to try and find some work for The Link. We barely had enough money to get there — my wife and I had to take The Linkmobile to the Fort Worth flea market on a Saturday made up as The Missing Link and Sheena, and sell pictures of The Link to finance the trip. I walked around the market and shook hands with all the small kids. We made about $250, some of which got spent first on beer, wine and marijuana for me so I wouldn't run out during the trip.

Going back to Kansas City was not a happy return for any of us, considering the circumstances we left under the first time. We got a room at the Skyline Inn where most of the Kansas City wrestlers stayed, and were there maybe a month until the money got really bad again. I was driving 600 miles some nights to shows and not making any money, so one day Gail and I just packed up the truck, went to work that night and planned to leave right after the show for Jackson, Mississippi, where we had friends we could stay with. Jason didn't come with us, and my wife and I had been on the road about an hour when we looked at each other and both had the same thought: "We can't leave him there!" We drove back to the house where he was living with a friend and asked him "Do you want to come with us?" Jason insisted he wanted to stay so we went on to Jackson. I kept right on drinking heavily and smoking my marijuana. After a week or two we were getting on the nerves of the people we were living with, so we left them and stayed with another couple in Jackson for a few weeks.

I don't remember now if there was any grand plan to what we did during this period. Sometime in the late '80s the U.S. government offered people who had been living there as aliens for a designated amount of time the chance to apply for amnesty and become American citizens. We had been considering doing this because the jobs were disappearing and we were getting desperate for money, but as we got on the road I think going back home to Canada became another option. One day we went to the flea market in Jackson with the truck and me all made up as The Link to sell pictures and sign autographs. We only made about $180 that day but decided it was enough to make our way to Charlotte, where we still had friends. It took us a few days to drive to Charlotte and we didn't have anywhere to stay so we'd look for a 24-hour waffle house, park in their lot next to the dumpster for a semblance of safety and sleep in the truck. I almost don't want to tell you this, but toward the end of the trip we couldn't even afford to eat in the restaurants and had to scavenge from the dumpster for our food. But even during this low point, people still showed us some kindness. We were down to our last $20 of gas in the tank, with no money for food, when a trucker who was a wrestling fan spotted The Linkmobile and started honking. The Lady in Black got on the CB and told him The Link was in the truck, so the trucker asked her to pull over because he wanted to meet me. We all pulled off at the next truck stop and even though I was still acting like The Link and not talking, he bought me a breakfast of steak, potatoes and six eggs and talked to Gail while I ate.

When we got to Charlotte we stayed at Edie and Gene Anderson's house. Gene was a wrestler and had been part of the famous Minnesota Wrecking Crew tag team with Ole and Lars Anderson, but he'd had a heart attack by this time and was working in the wrestling office. (Gene's gone now. He died in 1991 of another heart attack.) We got there in September and asked if they would mind us staying for a few days. The days stretched into weeks, then months, even though the whole time we lived with them I continued to drink — I could always find a bar where people would be happy to buy a few rounds for The Missing Link in exchange for hearing inside stories and being able to say they'd met The Link — and smoke marijuana. Because I was avoiding reality in this way, I never stopped to think how lucky I was to have friends who helped us out during this time of hardship. Can you imagine letting an addict live in your house for four months? God bless both Gene and Edie for being so generous with us.

Besides our financial woes, my health was going into a serious decline. I was now nearly 50 years old, and had I been wrestling for over 25 of those years — abusing alcohol, marijuana and steroids for the last 10. It was starting to catch up with me. After we'd found our furniture stolen and things were at their lowest, my son said to me, "Well dad, as long as you've got your health," not knowing how unhealthy I was. He arrived in the Carolinas about a month later, being unable to find work in Kansas City or Texas, and saw the painful truth about how sick I'd made myself. I had gone off the steroids — not because I knew they were damaging my health, but because I couldn't afford them anymore — and as a result my weight dropped from 260 to 190 in a very short time, and I barely had enough energy to get off the couch. I was also experiencing a resurgence of the spondylitis and couldn't afford the pills for that either, so by the time we got to the Carolinas I was very weak and in a great deal of pain. I didn't even have proper shoes, just a pair of thongs and winter was coming on, so I ended up having to pawn my $300 watch for $25 (my wife had already sold all her jewelry in Kansas City) to buy a cheap pair of running shoes. Not having green cards, all we could look for was under-the-table work. I was in no shape to wrestle and anyway the main city in the territory was now Atlanta, where TBS was located. We were so short of money that one morning my wife and I lined up outside a building at 5:30 with a bunch of other men looking for work and were taken by car to a location about 15 miles away, where all we had to do was fill a wheelbarrow full of earth and move it about 25 feet. I was still sick enough that this job was too strenuous for me — my wife and I worked together all day and made $25 between us.

During this time, strangely enough, I never got angry at the situation I found myself in. My wife and my son in particular couldn't understand why, but they didn't know that all the time this was going on, I was saying the Lord's Prayer over and over to myself, about 25 times a day, which helped me keep my sanity. I learned that from Percy Pringle, who was famous for saying "Praise the Lord, thank you Jesus" whenever anything happened. Percy was a very spiritual individual and he taught me a lot about keeping the faith and believing in God.

We finally made up our minds to return to Canada and left Gene and Edie's ten days before Christmas 1988. Jason had started a factory job in Charlotte and was beginning to meet people and get into a good lifestyle again, so when we told him "We're going back," he wasn't too happy. He actually made us stop the truck on the way there, yelling, "Let me out of this truck, I'm not going," but eventually he changed his mind and we drove the remaining 1,000 miles home straight through, crossing the Peace Bridge in Buffalo with nothing but The Linkmobile, the clothes on our backs and $26 to our names. I had a small 99-cent bottle of Thunderbird in the back of the truck I had been saving for when we crossed the border, and I cracked it open in celebration once we arrived at my brother-in-law's house.

CHAPTER TWELVE

Recovery

When we got back to Canada we stayed with my wife's brother for a couple of weeks, with the idea to make a little money then head out west to Stu Hart's Stampede Wrestling in Calgary — not knowing that it was on the verge of folding too, just like everywhere else. That idea was quickly abandoned, and we decided to stay where we were and try to put down roots again. We went back to Hamilton and found ourselves a hotel and eventually, an apartment. I didn't think about this at the time, but I see now that I was very lucky that we had old friends and family and a familiar place to go back to. The life of a wrestler is so transient that a lot of people never get a chance to put down any roots at all. I had my mother, my old friends, the relationships I'd formed when I was a responsible local businessman and my fans.

We still had The Linkmobile, and my son and I wrestled at local indie shows while my health was holding up — at the Hamilton Kiwanis club, for the CWA (Ricky Johnson's promotion) — just small shows. I tried going back to the Toronto booking office, but Frank was dead, his nephew Jack Tunney had taken over and Maple Leaf Wrestling was just a branch office of the WWF by now. When I got there they had a big truck out front unloading WWF merchandise to be put in Jack's office across from Maple Leaf Gardens. I offered to help unload the truck and hoped to talk Jack into hiring me for a few shows, but he wanted nothing to do with me. I heard him say to Eddie Tunney, "Give him 200 bucks and tell him to get lost." You could always count on Jack to have something nasty to say to everybody. He used to tell me not to jump up and down in the ring at the Gardens, because he didn't want the fans to know there were springs under it. Why anyone would have cared if they had known was never explained.

After we'd been home about a year, I landed a job working as a police escort for the Halton Region Police Services, picking up prisoners in custody at correction centers, detention centers, group homes and police stations and escorting them through the judicial system. Working as a police escort was a relatively short period in my life but even to this day I am so grateful for those two years, because it was a much-needed — but far from easy — turning point in my life. The way it happened was I had applied for a job with a security company, and needing a reference, had dropped into the HRPS HQ in Oakville, where I had heard an old friend was working as an executive officer to the Chief. He and I had been lifeguards in Burlington together. After many years of not seeing each other, he welcomed me with open arms, listened to the story of my past life and knew that I needed help to go in a new direction, especially spiritually. About two hours later I walked out of his office, after sharing my feelings for the first time in many years, with a feeling of serenity.

While I was there he encouraged me fill out an application to be an escort officer. His signature as a reference was very important, and this led me to another friend in the HRPS, a sergeant, who gave me a reference as well. The process moved quickly and within two months I was working as a sworn-in escort officer. In the course of my work I spent many quiet hours talking to my young charges, learning about their thoughts, ideas, problems, habits and their positive dreams about what they would like to do in life. I found out that young offenders were generally first incarcerated around the age of 14 years, and keep coming back until about age 18 to 20. At this age they lose interest in being there and being around the new, younger prisoners (or "being around losers" as they put it) and they definitely do not want to come back. They also begin to tell the younger ones to smarten up, because "it ain't worth it."

Hearing them talk like this made me realize that most of these kids probably could have turned their lives around if given the chance, but had been prevented by their circumstances from finding a better way. I began to think that if there was some way to give troubled young people some direction, and the opportunity to put their hands on an interest or activity that would make them more responsible, society as a whole could benefit from their input. This was when I first conceived the idea for the Critical Link Youth Services, which I envisioned as a special village or self-contained community like the Girls and Boys Towns in the United States, where at-risk kids could get away from negative influences, learn life skills and develop character and a sense of responsibility. Whipper Watson and I had discussed doing something like this when we were working together, and I never forgot about it. I also felt doing something like this might be a way to redeem myself after losing my way and letting down the many people who had acted as mentors to me and taught me responsibility when I was young.

I felt like I was up the first rung of my return from the bottom — I was enjoying my job and had a great boss, but unfortunately addiction wasn't finished with me yet. I had been with the police department about 18 months when the craving for marijuana started to come back. I can't say for certain why. Possibly once the stress of extreme poverty and homelessness had eased, other unfinished emotional business began to resurface. I may have been having trouble adjusting to being out of the spotlight after so many years in wrestling. When you've been a star, and living that life of constantly being on the road, it can be very difficult to ease yourself back into normal life after so many years of being worldly, even if you still have the people who knew you before that life to help you out. Finally I said to myself, "I can't do this any longer or I'll be the one who ends up behind bars." So I had to quit the job and with the help of a friend who was a high-profile businessman I went into rehab. You can't just show up and ask to be treated — you have to go to a doctor, there's meetings you have to attend — and within a month I was admitted to the 28-day residential program at the Donwood Institute in Toronto, part of the Centre for Addiction and Mental Health, which specializes in the treatment of substance abuse.

I actually enjoyed the time I spent at the Donwood. They take you from wherever you are in your addictions and make you extremely healthy. It was also very positive wanting to go rather than being told to go there, because it makes a big difference in the result. They test you for drugs and alcohol while you're there, and some people bring stuff in with them and get kicked out the same day before they've received any treatment. I went in with the attitude that my life had become unmanageable and I wanted to change it, so I was motivated to find a better way. To me the Donwood became the greatest place and I wish I could go back every year for a little vacation, because while you're there you feel great and they keep you busy. It was just like school. There are five classes a day with 12 people to a class, and you have maybe three classes in the morning and two in the afternoon. Sometimes you were in a big auditorium and other times it was relaxation classes. There's some sharing too, at anonymous meetings. I learned lots of things about myself there. And I still haven't learned everything about myself. When I got out of the Donwood, I began attending a 12-step program to further the process of recovery.

Part of my education about addictions was learning exactly what I had been doing to my body all this time. This information later became a section of my speeches that I call "They Didn't Tell Me." I also tell people that the first letters of steroids, alcohol and drugs spell out "SAD," because that's how you'll end up. The most important thing to remember is that addiction to alcohol and drugs is a physical allergy coupled with a mental obsession and if you can't stop it ends one of three ways: jail, insanity or death. Some of the side effects of alcohol abuse are dehydration, delirium tremens (temporary disorientation), trembling, convulsions/seizures, malnutrition, pancreatitis (an inflammation of the pancreas, which controls release of digestive juices and insulin), cirrhosis (hardening) of the liver, blackouts (no memory of what happened while you were drinking), depression, disrupted sleep, general uneasiness and stress. Side effects of marijuana use include paranoia, laziness, depression/thoughts of suicide, distorted thinking and cancer.

People take steroids for different reasons than they use recreational drugs — to make their bodies bigger, stronger and faster — but there is no reward for the steroid abuser either. Taken over the long term, they will destroy your body. The side effects of steroid use can include: mood swings, increased aggression, violent rage, hair loss, voice deterioration, liver cancer, ligament and tendon injuries, water retention, acne, elevated liver enzymes, elevated cholesterol, atherosclerosis (artery blockage), heart attacks, compromised immune system, epiphysel closure (advanced aging of long bones), cholestasis (obstruction of the gall bladder) and jaundice (yellowing of skin and eyes due to excess bile from malfunction of the liver, which can also affect digestion). Due to the irregularities steroids cause in hormone production and release, men can experience testicular atrophy (because the body stops producing its own testosterone), infertility, impotence, prostate gland swelling, breast growth and an increased tendency to promiscuous behavior. Hormonal side effects for women may include female hirsutism (masculine hair growth), a deepening voice, menstrual irregularities and breast shrinkage. Needle use can expose users to risk of infections, hepatitis and AIDS.

Once I began cleaning up, I saw that my desire to help young offenders get back on the right path could be extended to helping all young people avoid dead-ends like alcohol and drugs. I remembered my youthful desire to be a public speaker, which came back to me after I started going to 12-step meetings. In 12-step programs people get up to speak about their problems with addictions, sharing their experiences with the group, and after I'd been in it for a little while they gave me a chance to tell my story. I got more comfortable with talking about my addictions in front of a group, and in August of 1992 decided to start acting on my plans to help young people by applying to be a volunteer in the Young Offenders unit at the Hamilton-Wentworth Detention Centre. I was approved and began speaking to young offenders in group homes and jails based on my experiences. I also began to gather information about obtaining funding to start my Critical Link program for troubled youth.

From there I decided to try going into the schools, to reach the kids who hadn't gotten into trouble yet. I went to the vice superintendent of the Halton Region schools, who was the father of a friend from my youth who'd loved wrestling, and they had both watched me wrestle. It was a shoe in the door, and all the schools in the district opened to me. I was very successful as a speaker, especially with the kids, and because I came to really enjoy it, it was easy to do a good job. I would hear afterwards from the teachers and principals that the students would still be talking about my presentation days later, were going home and telling their parents about it, and some of them were even worried about me and hoping I'd be OK. I can't tell you how important kids are to me, helping them to make the right choices and telling them the truth about what steroids, alcohol and drugs can do to your life. The response of the kids showed me that I could put myself over with an audience without wrestling — though I have to say I think it was partly my wrestling experience that helped me communicate when I was speaking. Even when I was The Missing Link and didn't talk, all wrestlers learn to use body language and non-verbal cues to get the attention of a crowd.

That same year I met up again with my old friend Dean Walker, who had helped me get the job at Underwood-Olivetti so long ago. While Dean didn't say anything at the time, I know he was shocked by my appearance. The last time he'd seen me I'd been in my early twenties, in the full flush of health, and I knew I looked very old, and tired and beaten down to him now. Dean was at something of a low point in his life then too, so he understood how I felt. He was a filmmaker and had been trying for several years to get a movie script approved but wasn't getting anywhere, so we felt an instant connection in terms of being able to talk about feeling stuck and answering the question, "What do you do next?" Dean listened to my story and was the first person who encouraged me to write a book about my life, and for that I will always be grateful to him. He gave me a goal to strive towards when I was feeling lost. By the way, Dean is now a successful independent producer of sports programing in the U.S. and has done work for the Fox and NBC television networks — which goes to show that you don't stay at the bottom forever.

In late 1992 my wife and I moved into a house on the lake side of the Beach Strip in Hamilton, and my son Jason decided to start an open-air wrestling school in the backyard. I was doing a lot of speaking engagements and trying to write my book, but sometimes I would go out and give him a hand, lend the benefit of my own experience, so to speak. The school did very well, eventually moving downtown to a warehouse on Sherman Ave. Somewhere I have pictures of a very young Adam Copeland and Jay Reso (Edge and Christian) — both future World Champions — at one of Jason's shows. Harry Demerjian (Ref Harry D) was our referee. Another of Jason's more famous students was Sean Morley, better known to today's wrestling fans as Val Venis. I remember Sean very well — he came all the way from Peterborough to train with us. He was a nice guy to have around, never caused any trouble, picked up professional wrestling moves very quickly and he certainly looked good in the ring. Sean was also extremely quiet and shy at first, and no one would have guessed he'd be able to play a flamboyant character like Val Venis back then. I can't take any credit for training Sean though, because Jason was the one who went in the ring with him over and over and over again.

*   *   *

I did my best to stay busy, work on my recovery and keep on the right path, but there were more physical and mental health issues from my years of addiction coming to the forefront. At the end of May 1993 I began experiencing symptoms of anxiety and depression — tearfulness, excessive sleeping, low energy and loss of interest in activities that I enjoyed, like going to the gym — and I had to be hospitalized for a month. The doctors prescribed anti-depressants, a tranquilizer for my anxiety symptoms and because they thought I might be bipolar (manic-depressive) as well, lithium carbonate. I was also sent for a CT scan of my abdomen after a physical examination and it revealed a mass on my right side that was found to be a kidney tumor.

I had cancer.

I can't say for certain if any of the substances I abused caused the tumor, but long-term steroid use is known to cause both kidney damage and cancer. Surgery was scheduled for the end of July and I was discharged from the hospital with all the medications they'd prescribed for me, plus pills to help me sleep at home. The kidney tumor was successfully removed the following month. My physical health recovered but I was still experiencing a lot of mood swings, and I began going for marriage counseling and individual psychotherapy.

I have a tendency to get very down on myself when I think about how I allowed addiction to take over my life, wallowing in what we call "the poor me's" in 12-step terminology, but I guess maybe I should give myself some credit because even while I was going through these cycles of illness and depression, I was always trying to make a positive effort for the good. I joined the board of directors of the Canadian Council on Substance Abuse for a three-year term. I made an effort to get publicity in the Hamilton and Burlington papers for my speaking engagements and because of my long connection to the area I got a talent agent who helped me get parts on TV shows. I played a wrestler on the YTV series *Maniac Mansion* (featuring comedian Joe Flaherty of SCTV fame) who had to teach a large, childlike fellow that wrestling was in fact predetermined (you will never hear me call it fake!) and I was also on several episodes of *Due South*.

I continued to wrestle occasionally at small shows and I am indebted to my good friend Ref Harry D for reminding me about the following story. In April of 1994, Harry convinced me to let him come up and referee a show in Timmins (Shania Twain's hometown) where The Link and Jason Sterling were going to wrestle. The show was actually a two in one day shot, and it was being run by Bill Eadie (Axe of Demolition, Masked Superstar). The main event was Jake "The Snake" vs. Greg "The Hammer" Valentine. Also on the card were Mr. Hughes, Cousin Luke and Shane Sewell. It was a 12-hour drive up there, hauling the wrestling ring with us, and I was on Jason's case all the way up, trying to build up heat for our match. I did a trick I learned from Whipper Watson, that he used to do to me all the time when we were driving together. I'd get distracted, look out the window at a house or some trees, then Whipper would call my name, I'd turn around and his big fist would hit me in the face. We call that wrestling *kibitzing*. So as I was driving I would wait for Jason to look the other way and extend my fist, then quickly call Jason and when he turned around he was greeted by The Link's fist. Several of them were good ones, as Jason turned around really fast.

Once we arrived and dropped off the ring, we went to the hotel to meet all the boys and found out Jake "The Snake" and "The Hammer" would not make the show. Bill called star after star to fill the void, but couldn't get anyone and said that other people would have to work a couple of times. The crowds for both shows were great. The first show was over 2,000 strong and attendance for the second one only a few hours later was 1,700 plus. We gave them a great show and they were ecstatic. I got to work five times throughout the two shows, but the match of the night was The Missing Link vs. Jumpin' Jason Sterling. The fight from the truck would now continue in the ring. We had discussed the match previously — it was agreed I would do what we called "Link shit," Jason would get a comeback, but in the end the scientific style of Jumping Jason would lose to the barbaric Link.

As I entered the ring rubbing my hands, I smiled at Harry

while he checked my boots. He told me the opening spot Jason wanted to do and I said, "No. Tell him to lock up with me." Harry looked at me and said "What?" I repeated "Tell him to lock up." Harry told Jason, who responded with angry disbelief — he was already mad at me for all the business in the truck coming up. As the bell rang and we locked up, Jason started swearing at me, but I just smiled as we exchanged holds. I started to do Link antics and then The Link started to use armbars, wristlocks, and then a leg hold. Jason called Harry over to check him and said to Harry, "What the hell is he doing? He is The Link. Tell him to do Link shit." Harry relayed the message and I grunted back "No." The boys in the dressing room had been watching through the curtains because they knew what I was going to do and all of them were crying with laughter at this point.

The scientific Link continued to annoy Jason as the match progressed. Jason continued to complain to Harry and curse at me. "Harry, come here. Tell him to do some Link shit and let's go home." I locked up with Jason again, rolled him up and went into a figure-four. Harry said, "Ten minutes, guys." I sent Jason into the ropes and got him into a bear hug. He said, "Dad, I am going to kill you." The Link replied by slamming Jason 1-2-3 and the match was over but never forgotten. To this day we continue to laugh about it, and once in a while I get Harry to repeat, "Do some Link shit, Dad."

During 1994 I continued to do speaking engagements and I registered the Critical Link as a non-profit corporation and applied to the federal government for a charitable registration number. But I was still dealing with the side effects of my many addictions, including the bipolar state first identified the previous year by the hospital doctor, which was worsening. Bipolar disorder is also called manic-depression and while the exact cause is not known, there is thought to be a genetic predisposition in some individuals. It is often found in people who have drug and alcohol addictions (though whether addiction is a cause of bipolar disorder or a result of a person trying to self-medicate the condition with alcohol and drugs has not been determined) and it can also be triggered by steroid use. It causes a person to swing between two extreme mood states: mania, which is characterized by excessive energy and euphoria, grandiose and impulsive behavior (spending sprees, promiscuity, aggressiveness), ideas coming "a mile a minute," little need for sleep, unrealistic belief in your own abilities and denial that anything is wrong. The manic state is followed by depression, which feels all the worse for the energy of what preceded it. Your mood goes from euphoric to sad and anxious with feeling of guilt, worthlessness, pessimism, heavy fatigue, loss of mental focus, restlessness, sleep disturbances and sometimes thoughts of suicide. The manic phase can feel good at first, but as things in your head seem to move faster and faster, irritability and mental confusion set in and you feel frightened, out-of-control and trapped and can lash out at friends and family. And when the depression hits, you feel like there's an overwhelming burden of despair and failure pinning you down, and ending your life starts to look like the only way to stop the pain for yourself and the others around you.

My first attempt at suicide was in June of 1994. I took an overdose of one of my anti-depressants and I was hospitalized again. I didn't realize the dosage wouldn't be lethal, but the amount I took could have caused permanent damage if I hadn't sought treatment in time. I recovered from that attempt but the thoughts of suicide continued to haunt me. I continued to see doctors for help with depression and suicidal impulses, and they tried different medications — but it wasn't enough to stop me from going back to marijuana after five years of being clean, to try and ease some of the pain I was in. I have managed to stay sober for 15 years now, with no desire to ever pick up alcohol again, but I am still tempted to smoke pot to assist me in coping with the stresses of my life. You may wonder how I am able to fight one addiction so strongly but have to battle with another on a day-to-day basis. I can only compare it to a wrestling opponent. Some matches go very smoothly, just right, while with others nothing works the way you intend it to. I have grown to dislike even the taste of alcohol but pot not only tastes good, the high I got from it was like nothing else. The first high you get is incredible, and you continue to chase that feeling with each subsequent hit — but you never get there. This search for a higher high leads a lot of people to more serious street drugs. I was just lucky that my desire for the high never led me to anything harder.

Marijuana came back to me in the form of a young dealer I befriended, who would ask me to drive him around (because he didn't have a car) to pick up bags of pot to sell to his friends, get me to buy him coffees, food or ask me to front him the money to buy more dope. I did it to assure myself a constant supply, and smoked myself right back into the hospital after several months. It was one relapse too many for my wife.

My wife hadn't gotten involved when I went into recovery. We had tried marriage counseling and joined a Bible study group, but what she really needed was one of the 12-step programs just for families and friends of the addict, to help them learn how they have been enabling the addiction and what changes to expect when the addicted partner goes into recovery. She never did that, so the changes in our relationship when I stopped drinking and smoking marijuana scared her and made her think I didn't love her anymore. That may sound strange, but addictions don't happen in a vacuum. The addict's immediate family and close friends become partners in the addiction when they shield the addict from the consequences of his or her actions, and in 12-step programs that's called enabling, or sometimes co-dependency. You've already seen plenty of evidence of that — my wife never asking where I'd been when I didn't come home, driving me around so I could smoke pot before and after matches and not asking to be paid for her work as my valet. Enablers have to feel needed, and when the addict starts to recover and doesn't need their protection anymore, that can be threatening. Partners who enable addictions always think they are acting out of love — that if they just love the other person enough it will make the addiction go away — but all they're doing is removing any motivation for the addict to change and getting themselves mired even deeper in a destructive pattern. It's also quite common for the partner of an addict to resist looking at their own role in the addiction. They figure they've done enough work already trying to support the other person, and it can be hard to face the fact that they cooperated in their own victimization to a degree. And my wife had plenty on her mind without worrying about me any more. She had a demanding job (she became a visiting homemaker when we came back to Canada), plus trying to cope with my health problems and her own unresolved emotional issues from the turbulent final years of my career.

After I was hospitalized again near the end of 1994, my wife was advised by health professionals that she should leave our marriage for her own good, and in January of 1995 she moved into her own apartment. It was supposed to be a trial separation, so I dealt with it by telling myself she would come back to me eventually and tried to carry on. If nothing else, please understand this: I am not angry at my wife for leaving me. I was never angry at her. I have a lot of guilt and remorse about how I took advantage of her in our relationship, but you can't redo the past. She deserves a medal for putting up with me, taking care of me and standing by my side all those years. And she was good to everybody, not just me. Nobody had a bad word to say about Gail — everybody liked her — and I can't begin to apologize for all the things I did. She was my co-dependent, she looked after me, took the blame for all the accusations I threw at her on a daily basis, until finally she'd had enough. And I can't blame her for that, because most wrestling couples don't stay together as long as we did, especially when there's substance abuse in the marriage.

It wasn't just large things I did to her, there were plenty of small things — it's hard now to think of all the mistakes I made. I realized recently that my first addiction wasn't alcohol or marijuana at all, but other women. I've said that my mother brought me up to not lie or steal and I didn't, but on the other hand, from the first day I began wrestling I started stealing other men's wives, girlfriends and daughters and giving myself free rein in the direction of lust and immorality. This was one big lie to my wife throughout our marriage. I recall her often saying to me, "Dewey, you're a good man," so there must have been some things I did along the way that were good. But if I'm being completely honest with myself, they were probably things I did for my own selfishness, giving because I expected to receive more in return. And I have no way of making that up to her, except to admit that everyone has a breaking point and living with my addictions finally pushed my wife to hers. Gail had a lot of her own demons — she had a much rougher childhood than mine, and until she met me, I don't think she'd ever felt loved by anyone. And I believe that's why she stayed with me so long, far longer than another woman might have.

A few months after Gail moved out, she went back to Florida because she missed the warm weather after living in the southern United States for so long. That should have been a message that our separation was going to become permanent but I stayed in denial, still believing she would come back to me in the end. We did eventually divorce, which made me very unhappy. I was also in denial about the fact that my wrestling career was pretty much over, though I kept trying to stay somewhat involved. I went to Japan in 1995 to wrestle as The Missing Link for a promotion called WAR, run by a young man named

Tenryu I had wrestled a lot in the Carolinas. Tenryu was a former sumo wrestler who went into pro wrestling — I was one of the fellows who taught him professional wrestling — and had worked for Giant Baba's company before branching out on his own. In the mid-'90s there were 18 companies running in Japan, so the money wasn't nearly as good as it had been in the '70s and '80s when there was just a few. But I went anyway, even though I was out of condition. I have videos of those matches and when I watch them I cringe at how out of shape I look. However, most of the other guys were on the chunky side so I don't suppose I looked too bad next to them. I'd still like to go back to Japan again if the opportunity arises.

When I did my talks at schools and community groups, one question I always got asked by the big and small, old and young, was "What was your toughest match?" This question always stumped me. I would think in terms of physical opponents, a career spanning 44 years, hundreds of cities and many other countries, and nothing would come to mind. But about halfway through writing this book, I finally realized that my toughest match has been my recovery from addiction, and in particular the years after my wife left me, because then I had no choice but to face the consequences of all my mistakes.

After my wife left, the progress of my recovery got very rocky. It was a case of "one step forward, two steps back." I left the board of CCSA in 1996 when my term was up. The board's main function was deciding what information would go into a national database of drug and alcohol research, and I got the feeling they weren't all that interested in having input from a former user. They also weren't interested in talking about steroids at all. I kept on trying to get start-up funding for the Critical Link, but when the time came to go make my pitch I would sink into a depression and cancel the meeting. It didn't take long for people to stop taking me seriously.

Here and there I wrestled in small-town shows that wanted a former "big-time" wrestler to draw a crowd and paid me some much-needed dollars, but I was having difficulty staying motivated to go to the gym, let alone training hard to maintain my physique, and so I would turn to that wonderful high and escape everything. I could be good for a while and save $1,000 and then it would be gone in three months, all spent on marijuana. It was only when the high wore off and the sickness would return I would be reminded again of what little I had left and what I used smoking pot to forget.

I made my way down to what we call "the bottom" in recovery, that point when addiction has taken over your life and taken away everything that was good about it. I would get suicidal and sit around imagining dramatic ways to end my life, like pouring gasoline over myself and lighting a match, because that seemed like a better alternative than to go on living. In five years I had six different trips to area psychiatric facilities to try and regain control of my mind and my life. I noticed after each successive bout with marijuana my motor skills, eyesight, speech and physique would deteriorate just a little further. The cycles kept getting shorter too. At first I would smoke for three months on, be clean for three months, but towards the end it would only take a couple of weeks before the bipolar state would kick in and I would lose my motor skills to the point where I was physically unable to smoke even one joint. I was also a horrible person to be around when I was using, constantly complaining about my life, my wife and sons, and a lot of my friends got fed up with me. I'd try once in a while to get someone to help me write a book too, but I'd pressure them too hard or lose interest again when I went on another marijuana binge.

I did some extremely stupid and self-destructive things during this time. If anything proves that being hooked on marijuana is not worth it, these next few stories will. I had moved in with a female friend and after several months being clean and feeling good, I took advantage of her being away on a cruise to go on a three-day marijuana binge. It was the middle of winter and one of those nights I got up at 2 a.m. and decided to go for a drive. I went outside in my underwear, no shoes or shirt on, to get into the car but couldn't find my keys — so I started using a crowbar to try and open the door. This was an Oldsmobile I had just bought and spent extra money getting a gorgeous new paint job for it, but now I was kicking it in anger, denting the entire driver's side and smashing in a window trying to get it open, and my neighbors called the police because I was scaring them. Two officers showed up — one of the constables was quite young and I shoved him around jokingly, saying, "Yeah, you're just doing your job." I was lucky that having been a police escort for a couple of years they knew the condition I was in and that I wasn't really a threat to anyone except my car, so they didn't take me in. They eventually settled me down and I went back in the house.

Another time I took a trip to Montreal with the same female friend, because we had been given a complimentary weekend at a five-star hotel. After dinner I said I was going to the lobby to pick up a "message" and she went upstairs thinking I would be back shortly and we were going to have a nice quiet evening in, watching TV and enjoying the luxurious atmosphere. I really went looking for marijuana and returned *seven hours* later, and by then she was completely frantic, being alone in a strange city and not knowing where I was or if I was returning. I had no excuse — I was just feeling good and wanted to feel better.

Some time after this incident I split up with my companion and moved out on my own, because some of my so-called friends convinced me she was "controlling" me, which really meant restricting my use of marijuana. I told her I wanted to be alone, but this idea was put into my head by the young dealer I talked about earlier, who wanted me to be at his beck and call to drive him around and buy things for him in exchange for providing me with free marijuana. During this time I got involved in a car accident. What happened was I was driving very slowly and a man came out of the bowling alley, ran past my car and then "fell" back into the bumper, as though I had hit him. The police were called but no charges were laid against me, as there were a number of witnesses who told the police it looked like the guy had done it on purpose. That should have been the end of it, but this guy was some kind of scam artist who had obviously done this before, and he hired a lawyer and sued me, saying I was drunk (when in fact I had not had a drink in 12 years). However, when the summons to appear in court arrived, I didn't pay any attention to it because I was under the influence of marijuana again. Since I didn't show up in court and even though there was a police report on the incident that said it wasn't my fault, the guy was awarded $10,000 in an insurance settlement. The way I found out about it was when my insurance premiums jumped from $67 a month to $284. If I hadn't been high I would have answered the summons and the evidence from the police report would have cleared me of responsibility. It was as much my fault as the scam artist's.

Once I was living on my own, it didn't take long to spend all my money on marijuana and stop eating because I had nothing left for food (and I didn't even care about that because I had marijuana). So, after I had been doing marijuana for several days without any food or water, my landlady called an ambulance because she noticed my car hadn't been moved for several days (I had no money for gas either). In the emergency room they found my ex-companion's phone number in my wallet and called her to come in at midnight, because she was the closest thing to next-of-kin I had then. When she got there I was in such bad shape the doctors wanted her to authorize them to operate on me and put in a pacemaker. She got very angry, and refused to let them operate, causing a big fight in the emergency room. She kept repeating "This man has overdosed on marijuana. He doesn't need a pacemaker. All you have to do is leave him in a room for two days, feed him properly, give him his meds for thyroid and spondylitis and he will recover." They made her promise to take responsibility for not allowing the operation. Well, within three days I was running on the treadmill in the hospital with no problems and they let me go home. You know, now there's a lot of talk about legalizing marijuana because it's not considered dangerous — well, you tell me. None of those doctors knew I'd been on a marijuana binge when I got to the hospital.

Afterwards my friend watched over me for several weeks as I began to get better. With no more dealer hanging around, I was eating three meals a day, going back to the gym and within three months after smoking my last joint I was showing a huge improvement in appearance and manner. My lips were no longer blistered, swollen and blue, my skin was no longer yellow, I was talking normally instead of "racing" like I did when I was high, I was dressing properly and being courteous and kind to people again. I got back together with my companion, and some time had passed when she sent me out on an errand, not knowing my dealer friend had called me the day before and given me some marijuana. I had a joint while I was driving (and this was another new car), thinking it was no big deal, but the weather was bad that day and I lost control of the car and smashed into the back of a van. I totaled the front end and the insurance company wouldn't pay for repairs, they just wrote the car off — so here I was again with no car, and facing another three to six months of recovery to get myself healthy again.

As you can imagine, my companion was very angry when this happened and we began arguing a lot about my marijuana use. She'd say, "Stay away from that dealer! You cannot smoke anymore, it costs you money and one day it's going to cost you your life." I would reply, "I don't pay for my marijuana, it's free. My dealer gives it to me." One day she answered, "It's not free; you pay ten times over for it," and listed the ways I was paying for marijuana:

- The wear and tear on two cars
- Gas to drive the dealer around: $25–$35 dollars every two days
- Food for myself and the dealer: donuts, coffee, muffins, chocolate bars
- Greatly increased car insurance premiums because I didn't show up for my court case
- The destruction of our relationship and my relationships with family and friends because of my unacceptable behavior and
- The risks to my health by not eating and getting in car accidents.

The last thing she said was that God must have kept me and the people I could have injured in those accidents alive so I could share these stories.

Well, maybe she was right after all. While I was still stuck on this addiction treadmill, I got a phone call from Greg Oliver of the SLAM! Wrestling website. He was doing a story on father and son wrestlers for Father's Day and wanted to do an entry on me for their online Canadian Hall of Fame. I was still clinging to the belief that if I could just get a book about my life finished I would be able to put the past behind me and move on. So I interpreted this call as a sign that maybe God was willing to give me another chance. I told Greg I needed a writer to help me with my life story. He said he was too busy, but his wife, who was a writer as well, might be willing to take on the project. They came to see me together, and she agreed to do it. That was a big step back from the edge for me.

I'm not going to say it was all smooth sailing once the project was begun that summer but without her patience, persistence and encouragement, I would never have gotten all this down on paper. I continued to struggle with my mental health and family issues during the process, but as I began to put the whole story together with Meredith's help and remember the good times that came before the bad, things did begin to slowly turn around for me. I started feeling like I could reclaim the person I was before The Missing Link and my addictions carried me so far from the right path. It didn't happen overnight, because I still wasn't finished with marijuana and bringing up some of the memories sent me right back to it again, but I persisted (with a lot of outside help) because it gave me a sense of purpose and of hope that I could get my life back on track.

* * *

I recently bought myself my seventh vintage Cadillac, a 1987 Fleetwood Brougham, which is silver like Sweet Daddy Siki's Rolls-Royce in the '60s. Sweet Daddy was one serene gentleman, for sure. He was my tag partner in Toronto for a long time. We would stand at the dressing room door to wait for the announcer to call us into the ring. In those days I would be a little nervous and for a joke would tap him on the shoulder from behind and say, "Are you nervous, Daddy?" He'd look at me and smile and answer me with a very deep, chuckling laugh, which meant he wasn't nervous at all.

I'm telling you this because while you're nearly at the end of my long journey from success to addiction to recovery, I feel like I'm starting all over again, and it seems fitting that I have a new-old car for this leg of the trip. I hope one day I'll be as relaxed about the future as Sweet Daddy was about getting into the ring.

It has only been in these past few years that I was working on the book that I began to look honestly at the issues behind my addiction, my personal character defects and how they were magnified by abuse of drugs and alcohol. That's an important distinction, you know. The substance abuse does not cause defects, it enhances the ones you already have. I know now that before I could write about my recovery I had to live it, which means really getting down to the roots of my character flaws. I've had several 12-step sponsors and friends work with me on pinpointing the defects I have to work on, and since I started really listening to people I have begun to face some unpleasant truths about myself.

I've learned that I have always been driven by my ego and the belief that everyone else was doing better than me, and that led me to worship my cars, my body, my clothes, and all the material things money could buy. When I started wrestling, fame began feeding my ego, and the addictions to women, steroids, alcohol and drugs followed. I can't really blame the wrestling business for what happened to me, because I enjoyed being a wrestler very much and the business was good to me for a very long time. I fell by the wayside because I let external forces — people, things and situations — control my feelings instead of trusting my own judgment. My ego demanded that everyone had to like me, and I'd try to manipulate their opinions by doing things like giving away cars that didn't belong to me for a dollar if I thought that would help. By the same token, if I did a favor for somebody else, it would only be because I wanted something from them in return.

My egotism also told me that I always have to be right, even if that requires being condescending to people who disagree with me, or making fun of other people to make myself feel good. Ego makes me want to be in total control of every situation and when people don't do exactly what I want I have temper tantrums. Everything has to be done according to my schedule and I get very impatient and rude if it doesn't happen exactly the way I want it.

On the other hand if someone asks me to do something I don't want to do, I'll pick a fight to distract them and give myself an excuse to walk out and go do what I want. Even my thoughts of suicide were rooted in ego. Once I had driven away everyone who was close to me, I had no one there to reflect my own importance back to me, and my sense of self was completely lost.

I have come to realize that for all my talk about how important family is to me, I haven't treated mine very well at all. I always demanded their attention and obedience to me but never wanted to give anything back. At the point I started seriously working on this book, my oldest son had basically given up on me and was off living his own life, my younger son had moved to the West Coast with his family, and I was still continuing the standoff with my mother that had begun so long ago. She was very worried about my health, but I was still so full of ancient resentment that I couldn't see her concern was born out of love. When I had spent all my own money on marijuana on one of my downward spirals I would go to my mother for more money, she would say no and I would get angry at her for refusing enable my addiction, wallowing in the old anger I was still harboring at her for divorcing my father so long ago.

Before I could make peace with my mother I had to resolve my feelings about my father once and for all, so about three years ago I spent a couple of days just sitting by his grave on a folding chair, telling him everything that I hadn't when he was alive. I remembered what I learned in recovery about the state of insanity drinking creates in the mind and realized that my father was in that same state when he used to make the accusations against my mother that made me blame her for divorcing him. That knowledge created an opening for me to let go of my anger at my mother. I realized that by withholding my love and not letting my mother love me I had been stealing from her too. When I finally admitted to myself how wrong I'd been, I asked my mother for her forgiveness and she said immediately, "Byron, I forgive you." My mother never wanted me to be a wrestler but she's never reproached me for it either, and she didn't reproach me for the way I treated her all those years either. I am looking at my own son Jason now through my mother's eyes, as he just recently started wrestling as Son of Link, and I'm hoping he will not go in the direction of the downside of wrestling like I did. However, I will support him in his decisions, as I know now that I didn't listen either and had to learn the hard way.

Things aren't perfect for me yet, but they're getting better. I'm still taking some prescription drugs to keep my mind balanced, but it's better than the alternative. People are calling me now to make appearances at fan shows and even to wrestle as The Missing Link. In the past four years I've been to conventions in Texas and New Jersey and been amazed by the response from fans, especially considering I hadn't wrestled as The Link in either of those areas for at least 15 years, if not longer. I enjoy meeting and talking to the fans, but being asked to wrestle causes me a lot of anxiety because I get very afraid of going back down that road of destructive behavior and addiction again. Sometimes I forget how lucky I am to still be alive, given the way I abused my body as The Link, because a lot of my fellow wrestlers lost their fight with addictions. In the last 20 years in professional wrestling, 88 men and one woman have died before the age of 55 because of drug and alcohol abuse or health problems resulting from past abuse. In the last few years we've lost Davey Boy Smith, Curt Hennig, Miss Elizabeth, Road Warrior Hawk, and Eddie Guerrero. Like I keep saying, it ain't worth it.

I still feel sometimes like I let an awful lot of people down by going in the direction I did: family, friends, colleagues, my early mentors, the people I trained at my gyms, promoters who hired me and especially the people who helped me out when I had to start over again with nothing. But I've been getting back in touch with some of my old peers again and they've given me a lot of support. I've been told that there is enough good left in me for God to defeat the part that went bad, and that God has forgiven me. Now, I must forgive myself, and that's what I'm working on.

That's the story so far: the good, the bad and the ugly, just like I promised you. I hope you found it interesting. From now on I'm just trying to take life one day at a time, keep myself going in a good orderly direction (that's my definition of G-O-D), and maybe one day I will be able to make The Critical Link a reality. And while I'm glad people still love The Missing Link, he's no longer the center of Dewey Robertson's life. I don't want Dewey to be *missing* anymore. It took me a long time to find him.